FLASHBACKS

THE FLASHBACKS SERIES IS SPONSORED BY THE

EUROPEAN ETHNOLOGICAL RESEARCH CENTRE

CELTIC & SCOTTISH STUDIES

UNIVERSITY OF EDINBURGH

27–29 GEORGE STREET

EDINBURGH EH8 9LD

FLASHBACKS

FLASHBACKS

From Land to Rail

Life and Times
of Andrew Ramage 1854–1917

Edited by
Caroline Milligan and Mark A. Mulhern

in association with
THE EUROPEAN ETHNOLOGICAL RESEARCH CENTRE
AND NMS ENTERPRISES LIMITED – PUBLISHING
NATIONAL MUSEUMS SCOTLAND

GENERAL EDITOR
Mark A. Mulhern

Co-published in Great Britain
in 2014 by
NMS Enterprises Limited – Publishing
National Museums Scotland
Chambers Street, Edinburgh EH1 1JF

and the
European Ethnological Research
Centre
Celtic & Scottish Studies
University of Edinburgh
27–29 George Square
Edinburgh EH8 9LD

ISBN 978-1-905267-69-9

**British Library Cataloguing in Publication
Data**
A catalogue record of this book is
available from the British Library.

Cover design: Mark Blackadder.
Cover photograph: [front] Andrew,
Bella and family at Biel Gate, *c*.1920;
[back, photo.] Lachie and Andrew,
Edinburgh, November, 1916; [back-
ground] Andrew and his wife, Bella,
at Biel Gate, close to his retirement,
c.1914.

Internal text design by NMS Enter-
prises Limited – Publishing, National
Museums Scotland.
Printed and bound in Great Britain by
Bell & Bain Ltd, Glasgow.

For a full listing of related NMS
titles please visit:
www.nms.ac.uk/books

CONTENTS

From Land to Rail
Life and Times of Andrew Ramage 1854–1917

ACKNOWLEDGEMENTS

THE editors are greatly indebted to Andrew Ramage's great-grandson, Andrew, for all the work he had already completed on this project before the materials were submitted to the EERC. This work included scanning and then transcribing the original notebooks, sourcing and scanning family photographs, letters and other important documents and providing detailed notes on individual family members, including important wartime records. Thanks are also extended to Andrew for his support and guidance as work on the book continued and to Sheila Findlay who provided additional help with the footnotes.

Caroline Milligan and Mark A. Mulhern
EDINBURGH 2014

LIST OF ILLUSTRATIONS

1. Dodridge Farm, Ormiston, where Andrew was born in 1854.
2. Myles Farm, where the family moved to from Dodridge.
3. Harrow Hotel, Dalkeith.
4. Ecclaw Farm, of which Andrew said he was 'grieved to [go] where there was nothing to view but whins and heather and bleak mountains'.
5. Clints Farm, where Andrew went as a groom after leaving home for the first time.
6. Cockpen, where Andrew's mother was laid to rest.
7. Shepherd's cottage at Kidshielhaugh Farm. Andrew worked here for a term before heading off to live with his sister, Jane.
8. Andrew's sister, Mary, and her family, Ettrick, 1883.
9. Helen (Nell) Robertson (Andrew's sister-in-law).
10. Andrew's brother, James, with his family, 1887.
11. Newspaper advertisement seeking information about Andrew's brother, William. *Montreal Witness*, 1889.
12. Andrew and boy at Biel Gate, *c.*1905.
13. Andrew, Bella and family at Biel Gate, *c.*1920.
14. Mary and Roderick MacLean, *c.*1900, Andrew's sister and brother-in-law.
15. Agnes McLaren, Andrew's sister, with Elizabeth (Colina) and Mary, her daughters.
16. Alexander (son, Sandy) and family, Cheshire, *c.*1910.
17. Alexander, at post as a chauffeur, Cheshire, *c.*1910.
18. Alexander and Robert (son, Bob), *c.*1910.
19. Andrew (son) in Canada, *c.*1910.
20. (a–d.) Pages of a letter and envelope from Andrew to his son, Andrew, in Canada.
21. Andrew, 1913.

22. Retiral newspaper notice, 1915.
23. Letter from Andrew to his daughter, Jean, 6 August 1914.
24. Andrew and his wife, Bella, at Biel Gate, close to his retirement, c.1914.
25. (a–b.) Postcard home from Angus (son), Scots Guards, Caterham, 1910. (Angus is in the second row, second in from the left.)
26. Angus, Linlithgow Police, 1913. (Angus is on the right.)
27. Letter from Angus, September 1914.
28. (a–c.) Letter from Angus, October 1914.
29. Letter from the Scots Guards advising Andrew of the death of Angus on 26 October 1914.
30. Roll Call of Angus's battalion (2nd Battalion, Scots Guards) at Ypres on the morning of 27 October 1914 – the day after Angus was Killed in Action.
31. (a–b.) Condolence letter following Angus' death, from Revd Marjoribanks of Stenton Church, dated 26 December 1914.
32. William (son, Bill) with Territorial Army, 1909. (Bill is second from the right, back.)
33. (a–b.) Postcard from Bill to his sister, Jean. Lothian and Borders Horse, Haddington, August 1914. (Bill is the fifth seated person in from the right.)
34. Bill in army uniform, Edinburgh, 1916.
35. Robert (son, Bob) with Fraser's Squad, McArthur's Joiners, East Linton, 1912. (Bob is second from the left.)
36. Bob, RFC, 1915. (Bob is second from the left, front.)
37. Bob, RFC, 1916. (Bob is first on the left, back.)
38. Bob, RFC, 1916.
39. James (son, Jim), Military Mounted Police Christmas Dinner, 1915. (Jim is in the centre, under the window.)
40. Jim (front right), Military Mounted Police, c.1916.
41. Jim (extreme right), c.1917.
42. Jim, Military Mounted Police, c.1918.
43. Jim, Military Mounted Police, Roustchouk, Bulgaria, February 1919.
44. W. A. Ramage (Billie, nephew: back, left), Canadian Expeditionary Force, 1916.
45. Lauchlan (son, Lachie) in Royal Scots Uniform, with sister, Jean, c.1914.
46. Lachie (first on right), Royal Scots, 1917.

Images used in text

EDITORIAL NOTE

THE following editorial interventions have been made: Idiosyncratic spelling has been retained if the word or phrase scans well. In most instances where this is the case, e.g. byke for bike, the word/phrase appears many times. Other spellings have been changed to assist the flow of the narrative, e.g. changing 'of' to 'off' as appropriate. For such slight editorial interventions, no indication is given.

Square brackets have been used to identify more substantial editorial interventions. These occur in the following instances:

- To indicate that one or more words have been inserted or replaced in order to assist comprehension.
- To provide additional information. This may be to identify the relationship of the person being spoken of in the narrative, or may be to supply up-to-date county information to help the reader follow the geographical journey travelled in the book.

Punctuation has been changed or introduced to ease comprehension and help the narrative flow of the work.

Times, dates etc. have been standardised.

In the diary, Andrew often shortened names and places, e.g. Alexr for Alexander. However, these are given in full here.

Some words appear with various spellings in the original manuscript, e.g. 'canna' and 'cannae'. Where this is the case, the most easily comprehended spelling has been retained and applied throughout.

INTRODUCTION

ANDREW Ramage was born 15 February 1854 at Dodridge Farm in East Lothian and died 25 September 1917 at Dalmeny in West Lothian. His lifetime spanned a period of history which saw great change, both locally and internationally, and Andrew's own story reflected this.

Between 1889 and 1917, Andrew wrote about his life in a series of notebooks beginning with a memoir describing his early life in detail, before moving on to a more conventional diary. As he filled one notebook he began another, and we cannot say how many notebooks there were originally as most have been lost along the way: leaving us with just three for consideration in this volume. Andrew's descendants, recognising the value of the surviving volumes, scanned and transcribed the notebooks and presented them to the European Ethnological Research Centre, together with a large number of scanned photographs, letters and documents pertaining to Andrew and his life. Much of this work was completed by Andrew's great-grandson, also Andrew Ramage, and we are indebted to him for his dedication and attention to detail in preparing this material.

While we might regret not having the opportunity to read the full set of notebooks, the episodic nature of the narrative provided by the three remaining volumes takes us on a journey which is personal, rich in content and informative, and perhaps even, we might say, enhanced by their being only fragments of a far larger story. Childhood and old age are represented here, life and death are here, and so too are peacetime and wartime. All are represented in a highly personal way, allowing us to feel empathy with Andrew as we drop into his life at various significant points. It is certainly tempting to believe that, whether during a spring clean or a house move, when the decision was made to discard Andrew's notebooks, these three volumes were consciously selected from the others because they contained such interesting and poignant information.

Of the three surviving notebooks, the first contains the memoir (dated 2.11.1888) and Diary: Part I. The memoir and diary (dated from 4.11.1888) were written from opposite ends of the notebook and this can explain why the memoir finishes abruptly, mid-sentence. We can presume from this that it is likely the memoir continued in the next notebook (one of the missing volumes). The first notebook ends 2 April 1889. The second notebook (Diary: Part II) begins on 26 July 1914, so there are, we can surmise, many intervening volumes missing. This volume ends on 20 February 1916. The third surviving notebook follows on directly from the second, beginning 21 February 1916 and continuing up to the last entry on 21 June 1917. By this time, Andrew's handwriting has deteriorated significantly and he was clearly in poor health. He died only a few months later in September 1917.

Before we look at the three notebooks in detail, it is useful to say a little about Andrew's life in the period prior to 1888, when he began his memoir. In 1883 he was twenty-nine years old and living in Edinburgh. He was married, with three small children, and was working as a railway yardsman at the North British Railway (NBR) yard at Portobello. On 12 September of that year, he had an accident at work which resulted in the amputation of his right arm. The accident report stated that 'The yardsman, when running alongside [a] passenger train in motion at Portobello, tripped and fell with his arm in front of [a] carriage wheel, which passed over it'. The report concluded that a 'want of caution' on Andrew's part was the reason for the accident and so the responsibility rested with him. Unable to continue as a yardsman, the NBR moved Andrew and his family to Stenton,

East Lothian, where he was to be gatekeeper at the Biel road crossing of the London–Edinburgh rail line until his retirement in 1915. It was here that Andrew, now aged thirty-four and with six children, began work on his memoir and diaries. This may have been to help him pass the quiet hours at Biel, and may also have served to help him cope with the continuing pain and other health problems associated with his amputation. It is worth observing that Andrew was naturally right-handed and therefore he would have had to re-learn to write with his left hand following the accident.

The memoir is a powerful and engaging narrative. Andrew was reflecting on his own childhood and family circumstances from the time of his birth, until the age of about seventeen. It is a vibrant introduction to Andrew. He is writing as an author, and is doing so with an audience in mind. Indeed, he addresses us directly at one point when he says 'But, do not suppose, dear friend …'. His style is that of a story-teller and his various escapades are recounted with self-confidence and aplomb. He was fiercely proud of his father, and the importance of family is evident throughout. The early death of his mother, in 1868, took its toll on the family until eventually Andrew's father was forced back into service while the rest of the family were scattered around and about. Andrew had various agricultural tenures from the age of twelve, before moving into Edinburgh at fifteen. Here he worked first as a carter, and later as a horse-drawn lorry driver, and we read how the prevalence of alcohol and the separation from his family soon lead him into a somewhat dissipated life where drinking and having a good time were the order of the day. He declares himself to be very much his own man with strong opinions and morals, and also, latterly, a rather Godless, feckless one too. Alongside the tales of his own personal battles and triumphs, he gives us a tremendous insight into the life of agricultural workers during this period: the challenges of the term labour system and the vagaries of different employers; the difficulties of keeping the family together; the challenges of moving from community to community; the role of migrant workers; rural education; the agricultural calendar; and also the choices facing younger farm workers, especially at this time given the lure of work in the urban centres.

Dated just two days after the memoir, the opening diary entry reveals the mature Andrew to be a very different man. He was now settled at Biel and, evidently, returned to the church and Christian community. He was writing on a day-to-day basis and the entries reflect a focus on domestic matters. He and his wife, Isabella (Bella), had six children by this time, with four more to follow. His father was living with them, and being cared for by Andrew and Bella. This domestic focus is a constant for Andrew, and particularly understandable here as this was a traumatic time for the family. Andrew's father was in poor health (he died at home on 15 March 1889), while both his son, Duncan (Dow, aged eight) and his wife, Bella (who was around thirty-one at this time) experienced episodes of critical illness which took their toll on everyone. Despite this, Andrew's diary also reflects a continuing interest in the plight of the agricultural workers, especially the ploughmen, and there are several draft letters addressed to the newspapers included here which serve to demonstrate this commitment. Here too there are a number of poems which, like the memoir, tell us more about Andrew as a creative person. These are, for the most part, light in nature: often about exactly what is happening in his life at that moment, and these help us to connect more vitally with Andrew.

As the second notebook begins (Diary: Part II), twenty-five years have passed to Sunday 26 July 1914. Andrew and Bella were still working at Biel and the family had embarked on their own journeys, although sadly Duncan (Dow) had died in 1892 (aged eleven) after contracting meningitis. George and Andrew were already in Canada, and James would follow them after the War ended. Jean was working in domestic service, sometimes in Edinburgh and other times she would be at Biel with her parents. These were extraordinary times. Before long, six of Andrew's sons would be involved in the looming conflict that became the Great War. Two, Angus and William, were called-up immediately, Lauchlan (Lachie) joined in September 1914, and they were then joined by Alexander, James and Robert.

Sadly, Angus was Killed In Action, on 26 October 1914 at Gheluvelt, Ypres. This event, so early on in the conflict, must have had a tremendous effect on Andrew. Indeed we get a sense of this in the remaining diary entries, as we are struck by the to-ing and fro-ing of letters – and of people – which are recorded in the daily entries. Andrew frequently refers to the letters he has received from one or other of the boys, or of the letters he is sending off, and he often expresses anguish when he hasn't heard news for a few days or weeks. Through these short diary entries we are able to experience the sadness of losing Angus, and also the tremendous frustration of trying to find out what happened, and when. At this time there were several mail deliveries a day, and news was coming and going very quickly. But at other times, there is only an absence of news and of certainty.

During this period we move on to notebook three, which follows on immediately from the end of notebook two (20–21 February 1916). The War continues to be a constant backdrop to day-to-day life for Andrew and his family. Small comments and tiny details given here help us to understand more fully what it was like to live with war. Some topics we might have anticipated: fear for loved ones involved in the conflict; concerns regarding the availability of food, or services; zeppelin attacks. Others though, are quite unexpected. One that stands out is the fear of spies, and Andrew often mentions strange lights (as if signalling), and strangers (often with unfamiliar accents) travelling about the area, taking notes or photographs.

At the same time though, Andrew had other pressing domestic concerns. He retired in 1915 and had some agonising times looking for a new home for himself and Bella. Luckily, he was helped in this endeavour by his nephew, David Ramage, and the family moved to their new home on the Craigiehall Estate. Along with the War and domestic concerns, he also had money worries and persistent health problems. His writing during this period becomes more difficult to decipher, and he is obviously debilitated by pain, and also, perhaps, depression. The entries are more sporadic, sometimes with substantial periods of time missing. At the time of his death, on 25 September 1917, five of his sons were serving with the armed forces, and another two were far away in Canada. The last diary entry we have for Andrew is from Thursday 21 June 1917. Poignantly, his last words are 'No word from any of the boys abroad'. It seems a very appropriate sentiment to end on from a man whose family, as we see in his written record, were always at the heart of his life. As a reader, we can only feel privileged to have been allowed this insight into his life, and enriched by the detail he provides on the experience of our shared history. I believe that Andrew would have been delighted that his story has finally reached the audience he first addressed in 1888.

Caroline Milligan
EDINBURGH 2014

MEMOIR

Note Book
belonging to
Andrew Ramage
Gateman at
Stenton Level Crossing
East Linton

Andrew Ramage, 1910.

Andrew Ramage
2 November 1888

THE writer of this was the son of a farm servant who, at the time of the writer's birth, was imployed on the farm of Dodridge in the parish of Ormiston [East Lothian]. At which place he resided for the short period of three months, which place he left on the 26 May 1854 and removed to another farm near Tranent, called Myles.

At that time Myles farm was tennented by one Wm. Shiels[1] with whome my father did not get on very well with, he being of a very tyranical disposition and had no faith in a servants' honesty behind his back. As my father would not run and fluster in his presence, but kept on at his usual pace, he was often gauled by some very cynical expressions to which it is needless to allude.

One Dalkieth market day[2] [my father set off], it being [his] turn to go to the town with the sample bag. For in those days, farmers usually sent their grain to market in carts and had their sample carried into the Exchange where, after being sold and getting the address from the buyer, it was carted to the station and sent off to its destination the same day. The present day fashion is for the farmer to take only a small sample bag in his pocket to market, sell so many quarters[3] and post it on at the nearest station where his carts could go, say, four turns in a day. Or, by which plan, one man can ship as much grain with one pair of horses as four pairs could do taking it to market, standing in the market place till it was sold, and then again standing [in] turn at the station where you had often to wait on wagons being brought in. Well, my father, having got his sample carried in, and Mr Shiels selling early, he got a very good chance at the station, being among the first to arrive. So he came out to an inn at the station gate, called The Harrow, where the ploughmen usually got broth on the market days. Some of the inns in Dalkieth make kale[4] on Thursdays to this day and, as they are given grattis, they are well patronised and help to make the bad whisky sell.

So, my father, having got his kale and bap or roll finished, and drank the rest of his allowance in that same bad whisky, about a gill I think, he got out his horse and yoked the cart and went down the High Street to collect some parcells for his master at various tradesmens' houses. He also got some provisions to take home for my mother who always dealt in Dalkieth as she said it was the cheapest town in Scotland, having no burgh taxes to pay.[5]

Having got all his errand and congratulating himself on his success in getting so early through, my father went off whistling like a blackbird down the High Street, making for home and pictureing to himself the gladness on my mother's face when she saw him so soon, for this night was to be an exception. But [as] man proposes, God disposes. The fates were against him for he had not proceeded far till he was hailed by a publican standing in his door who came out after he had stopped and told him his master, 'Old Shiels' as he styled him, was in one of his rooms, drunk. And he would like [my father] to take him away home as he was annoying his customers – [Shiels] being a very quarrelsome man in drink. So my father went in and asked Mr Shiels to come away and go home in the cart with him, as the night was getting dark and wet. But he refused to stirr and ordered my father away home which he was nothing loth to do. But the landlord got some men and, just as [my father] was starting away, they carried out Mr Shiels and flung him into the cart where he lay for some time quite stunned by his uncerimonious exit. By this time my father, driveing as fast as he could, had got well out of the town [and was] proceeding down by the Lothian Bridge, which spans the Esk. When, all at once, he was caught by the back of the neck and dragged into the cart where Mr Shiels was – for he had been sitting on the front of the cart with his feet on the traivis. After he pulled my father into the cart he demanded to know if he thought he was a better man than him. But, as my father knew he was his master he did not want to have any rows with him, so he quietly shook himself clear and mounted his seat. He drove steadily on, only keeping his eye on his master who made several clutches at him but he always avoided him, till [Shiels] got drowsie with the drink and slept. Now, thought my father, he's all right. He'll sleep till I get him home. But again he was disapointed, for on passing the small mining village of Cowpits, [East Lothian] some young lads who were collected on the out-skirts raised a loud shout which roused up Mr Shiels, who swore terribly. Jumping out of the cart he [Mr Shiels] offered to fight the best man among them. The lads at first only laughed at him but as he was rather aggressive some on the out side of the crowd gave him a blow which sent him sprawling on the hard road. My father, meanwhile, got them advised not to punish him any fur-ther as he was the worse of drink and so hardly responsible for what he was doing. So, on getting him up and cleaning his face of the blood and dirt with which it was besmeared – for it was all scratched with his fall on the road – he got them to shake hands and assist to put [Shiels] in the cart again, and getting up beside him proceeded on his journey till he arrived at Crossgatehall Toll bar, where there was also a small inn.

Here, Mr Shiels who was by this time beginning to sober, told him to stop and bring him out a dram. But, no sooner had they stopped than the landlady came out, and seeing who was in the cart insisted on his coming in to warm himself on such a cold wet night. Running in she brought out a chair to assist him to alight. After getting out he ordered the horse to be stabled and fed, and my father to go to the kitchen and refresh himself at his expense. Mr Shiels went off with the landlady to join the landlord and some friends – where he remained for two houres amid song and clatter. When he came down to look-up my father with the cart he was as drunk as ever, but he was in good hands here [as my father] knew how to humour him.

When the cart was got out and all ready, the chair was brought out and they assisted him to mount and arranged the straw and bags to his entire satisfaction. And, after shaking hands, they all parted the best of friends. Well now, thought my father, perhaps we'll get home without any more nonsense. As he was in a good humour on parting, perhaps he will remain so till I can get him home. But, while he was yet thinking of getting him safely home, up starts Mr Shiels and accused my father of having 7£ belonging to him which he had missed while in the inn at Crossgatehall. And, he says, 'You must have took it off my person between there and Dalkieth'. At first my father thought he was only joking, or only making this an excuse for a row, knowing well he did not like him and would be only too glad of any paltry excuse to dismiss [him]. So he only told him he had no money of his and that perhaps he had only mislaid it, and would find it in some of his pockets [at] home. But Mr Shiels was persistant in his accusation and at last took [my father] by the cuff of his coat and dragged him into the cart again and swore an oath he would either shake it out of him or half murder him. So, as you may suppose, this fairly roused my father who had been trying all night to controle himself and now gave him a bot in the ear for his answer, and sent him rolling over among straw. Then, stopping the cart, he told him, if it was a fight with him he wanted, to come down to the road and fight like a man and not to be worrying at him like a dog whenever he turned his back. So they both got out on the road and set to work in a twinkling. My father was in too big a passion to fight and so got a knockdown a time or too which cooled him a bit and showed him his error – and the advantage he was giving his adversary. So he hung back and contented himself with defence which placed him in a better position and let the other man exhaust his strength on empty air. And, when he saw signs of him failing, he gave him a feller which sent him among the horses' feet and from which he did not come round for a few minutes, after which he asked to be helped into the cart and taken home. But, says my father, 'What about your 7£? Do you still accuse me of taking it?' 'Oh' says he, 'I speak to you about that tomorrow.' 'You coward', says my father 'If you dare to impeach me of stealing your money I'll give you in charges for your cowardly assault.' So off he drove home, where they arrived at ten o'clock – being six hours on the journey.

My mother was waiting up for my father, fully expecting him to be the worse of drink that he was so long in coming home, and [she] was distressing herself terribly till she heard his voice speaking in the stables. Then she knew he was quite sober. Whatever was the cause of his delay, she would hear in good time. So, after seeing Mr Shiels into the house and tending to the horse he came home and told his tale to my mother [from] when they both prepared to get the order to flit in the morning. But, when morning came my father got his orders to go to the plough with the rest the same as usual, which he did. About dinner time Mr Shiels came to my father. 'Sandy' says he, 'You and I had a row last night. Can you tell me what it was about?' 'You old two-faced villain. You know well enough what it was about.' 'Upon my word, Sandy …'. Says my father, 'Have you lost any money?' 'No', says he, 'No that I ken o.' So, my father says, 'That's all I care about it, for the rest you know as well as I can tell you all about it. So there is no more need of discussion.' 'Oh', says Mr Shiels, 'You seem to be very independent about it so I think the best thing for us both is for you and I to part'. 'Well' say[s] my father 'Have you any thing against me but my independence?' 'No', say he. 'Then', says my father 'I will leave you at the usual term[6] but not before, as I do not care to break my service and my character to please you, unless you are prepaired to pay me my wages up to that date.' 'So', say he 'If I am to pay you, I will have my pennyworth's out of you.'

So, they agreed to go on till the 26th of May when my father went further east in the county to a place called Garilton [Garleton], about three miles from the county town of Haddington, to be farm steward to a gentleman farmer, a Mr White. Here he had the whole management of the farm and the hireing and payment of the workers. [This] cost him many an anxious night learning to write and count as all the schooling he had got when a boy was six months one winter, he having to start work when he was nine years of age. But, with the help of some of my elder brothers, he suceeded in mastering the difficulty. All the rest was pretty plain sailing as he had long since, through bitter experiances, master[ed] all the practical detailes.

Here, things were more comfortable at home as by this time three of the oldest of the family were working and my father had a much better wage than ever he had as a ploughman. But do not suppose, dear friend, that we were in affluence. Because a family of nine is no joke to keep in thack and rape,[7] but [we were] just a little better than when he had nothing but his own hand darg to keep us right and tight.

Here my father got on pretty well for over the first year, although Mr White had found fault with him several times when he came on him unexpectedly and found him with his coat off, working. At such times he would fly in a passion and tell [my father] to put on his coat and find some one else to do it – he did not keep him for working, but only to see it done well. After being repeatedly found fault with, one day [my father] sent one of the men away to do some job that was urgently needed at the time and, as they were thrashing, my father intended looking after the engine himself, which this man usually did. But the engine keeper, not being pleased with this arrangement, went off to the master with his complaint. Mr White came to my father in a terrible rage about it and would not hear his explaination but ordered him to reinstate the man in his usual place, which he did, and [then] went and did the other job himself. When he had accomplished [that] he went off to Mr White and told him if he was going to support any body that went to him with a complaint, with out hearing both sides of the question, he would soon have plenty on his hand. How could [Mr White] expect him to have any authority, if he did not support him. And, since he had done so once he would never do so again as he would leave him on Saturday night, or now if [Mr White] would come and take over the books. This Mr White refused to do, and said he was sorrow for what he had done, now that the anger was off him. 'But,' says my father, 'You have taken my authority from me by your interfearance. Had you quarreled me by my self I would have thought no thing about it, but having done so before the rest of the workers they will always be coming to you with storys and complaints. So make up your mind for Saturday night.' So, after [father] payed the workers, he took up the books to Mr White and handed them over, and refused to stay.

After, there were some very bitter things said about the individual who was at the bottom of the row. And my father [told Mr White] that if it had been any one else who had taken the story to him they would not have got any cuttings, but that [White] dare not refuse him, for reasons best known to himself – but which the rest of them in the place knew a little about, though probably not the right way. But it was perfectly well known that [that person] had put away once and [Mr White] had to go and bring him back. All this put Mr White in a rage – as it was intended to do – and he gave him his wages and nottice to leave the house at Martimas, which my father promised to do.

I think my father was often sorrow about his hasty action in this case as it put my mother and all the family to a great deal of trouble and vexation and threw the older ones out of work for nearly all winter and caused two of my brothers to go to service and broke up the family circle so that we were never all under the same roof tree[8] again. In speaking of these times years after, he was wont to say, 'Aye, expeariance teaches fools, gin ye will to Cupar ye maun to Fife.'[9]

Now, as my father was out of a place, it behoved him to look about for some place to go, having, as I have said, to clear out at Martinmas. So he went off to Edinburgh on speck and fortunately met one Mr Stenhouse, an old master he had served before, who engaged him for his son who was taking the farm of Myles – which [father] had left [before], to be foreman ploughman. Here again my father came in contact with Mr Shiels. But, although he only remained in the same place up till Whitsunday term, he never would meet him or look in his face. If he had any thing to say, or any thing he wanted done, he always sent one of his sons to ask [Shiels] if he would do it as young Mr Stenhouse, my father's master, seldom came about the place, not getting possesion of the farm house until the Whitsunday term – which is not a very good arrangement of the incoming tennent. Here we stayed on for another year and here also my father was very comfortable.

About this time my adult brother George got married to a young woman called Margaret Robertson whose parents lived near Pathhead Ford [Midlothian] at a small house on the roadside called Burnside – there being a burn running in front of the house. It stands about a mile south-west of the village of Pathhead Ford. So, they started their married life at a farm called Blackshiels Mains, about two miles further south. But, as I do not intend to follow them further, here we will leave them, happy and contented.

Here, also, my third brother, Stephen, ran away and listed into the 71st HLI,[10] at that time stationed at Stirling Castle. Poor fellow, he fell asleep sitting on the edge of his bed in the stable loft sewing his trousers and the candle, being only stuck to the bed-post, fell down and set fire to some straws lying about. But, although he put out the fire himself without raising any alarm, in the morning the master, who found the smell, questioned him about it. And on learning that my brother had candle, he gave him his money and told him to go about his business or to go home to his father. His master was Mr Stenhouse, at that time farmer of Southfield, near Cramond Bridge [Drum Brae, Edinburgh] and father to my father's present master at Myles.

So, Stephen, for that was my brother's name, would not come home. He would rather [en]list, poor fellow. If he had only thought of the misery it was to cause him through my mother's grief he would have thought twice about it, for he was her favourit son. She went to Stirling and saw him away to India to help put down the mutiny.[11] Poor fellow, he got seven years of India before he got home again and got liver complant which helped to shorten his days. But I need not follow him further.[12]

On my mother coming home from Stirling, and telling my father the reason of his running away, my father wrote to Mr Stenhouse saying he might have let him know, either by letter or through his master, so that he could have come and taken him home, or found some other place for him as he was only a lad – being only sixteen years of age when he listed. But there the matter ended as [Mr Stenhouse] took no nottice of the letter.

So, my father left owing to this incedint and went to a Mr Wight at a place called Ormiston East Mains, [East Lothian] commonly called House of Muir – there being a small collier village of that name close by and the ploughmen's houses stood right in the middle of the village. And a rough and lawless class of people they were. Nearly all friend[s][13], and most of them were great poachers and drinkers. I have been in a good few towns since and, as far as my expearance goes, I have never seen any thing to come up to it for drinking and debauchery. I have seen a respectable married woman torn out of her bed by the hair of the head, and dragged down the street to the common drinking well and plunged in till she swooned – by other women – for no other reason than refuseing to drink a cohabit with them, and her husband sitting in another house laughing at them.

There was no policeman nearer than Ormiston and if any person made a complaint, or gave any information or evidence, they were half murdered. The first dark Saturday night. Here, I first began to take note of what was going on round about and here.

I first went to school [here]. Not very prommissing surroundings you will say, but poor people have to lye with strange bedfellows. This being a woman's school who had very little control of the bigger boys and, as the young always ape the older, I soon became one of the very worst. As the complaints reached my father I was soon packed off to Pathhead Ford to a man's school – a Mr Noble – and a vicious old tinker he was.

Here I had to walk four miles daily back an fore. The master's son went on a little white pony, and often he used to give me a ride behind. At other times, when he was on his dignity, he went past as if he did not know me. So, I soon turned. I would not go near him, but sometimes I used to run and catch hold of the pony's tail and draw it round and round till he was forced to come off and run after me. [Then] the pony would run off home and leave him to walk home, which we used to do in company after I had made him promise he would not touch me. A promise he rairely kept. But, as he was a good four years older than I, of course, I had to take that [in] good part. About this time I learned to smoke, as Bill – that was his name – carried a pipe on the sly [and] he encouraged me to get one also. And [he took to] hideing his in some hole in the wall, for he was terribly afraid of his mother who would have made his father belt him [if it was found], for she was boss and truley ruled the man. And, as truuly could it be said, the Devil ruled the woman for she never was content unless she was at war with someone. So you see, it was handy for him to get a smoke from me, and he used to steal tobacco from his father. But, as time went on an we got fonder of it I had to steal also – but I was not long in being found out. As my father only got a certain amount weekly he soon missed it, and my mother – searching my pockets – got pipe and tobacco.

Here I got on very well with my lessons for Mr Noble was a good school master, although few of his scholars had any love for him. So, for four years I went to Pathhead until Mr Wight, whose lease of the farm was out, he took another one away in Berwickshire. Here my father would not go with him at this time (although he went after), so we flitted from there to a place called Outerstone [Outerston, Midlothian] near the village of Temple. Here there was no-one to go to the school but my self from the houses – that is the ploughman's houses – so I did not care to go my self at first. For although I had been among so many and such a rough lot of boys and girls, still I was always shy to take up with strange people and this shyness has never left me all my life. I have always been slow to make new friends, and as slow to part with the old. Although, God knows, I have had few real friends. Well, in a few weeks, I struck up a friendship with the master's two daughters, one of whome was in my class at school – a Mys Willimina Brown. Well, Will and I, as she was called, stuck fast friends for the whole two years and nothing her sister, Jane –

who was two years older – could do or say could make any difference in [Will's] demeanure towards myself.

As for my self, many a fight I had for her and always, when
I could get a chance, I was with her. At last Jane told her mother,
and [Will] was not allowed to speak to me. Jane slapped my ear
for speaking to them, and then Willie used to write among the
snow on the road with her umbrella for me to read. When I was
first [to pass] I wrote to her, [and] so this infuriated Jane more
[and] she told her mother again. So, one Saturday when I was
running about the Mains, she cryed me inside to the kitchen and
asked me why I continued to anoy her girls going to school, and
[said] if I did not discontinue it she would tell my father. I said
I only annoyed one of the girls – who thought herself better than
me because I was not as well dressed as herself – and that if she
tried to take down her daughter's pride a bit, instead of
supporting her in her contempt of me, perhaps it would be better.
By this time she was so angry she could not speak. But her
husband, the master, who was in the parlor [and] had heard the
row – for I was angry and spoke loud – came in and said, 'Well
done my boy. And so you are as good as any of them are you?
Well, in my opinnion you are the best of the three. Never be
ashamied of your position. And you, Jane, I will send you where
you will find your equivalent and be looked down on as a poor
farmer's daughter, even as you are looking down on this boy
because his father is my servant and whose labour upholds that
bravery[14] you think so much of.' So, he sent her off to Edinburgh,
to a boarding school, and I never saw her again but at a distance.
Willie and I got on first class, and when it was a wet and stormy
day I went down to the big house and taught her her lessons for
the morrow and so [I] became to be great friends with the whole
household, which consisted of two sons and six daughters.

Here, also, I had two rare companions in two boys of the
house of Kinnear whose father was a ploughman. Many were
the rambles we had up on the Moorfoot Hill on Saturdays and
in the hollidays – pulling the blaeberries and crowberries which
grew in abundance on the southerin slopes of the [hill]. Usually

comeing home from those excursions laden with fruit, or sometimes following the burns for miles. Catching the trouts with our hands, and often getting a string of them that any Gala or Tweed angler would have been proud of. Some times also, especiallin in snow, we used to go a hunting of the rabbits which swarmed [the] young cover or plantation up in the moor, [from] where we sometimes had great dificulty in finding our way home.

Sometimes we got a few rabbits, but oftener we got our labour. But it was more for the fun and diversion that we went, as I dare not take a rabbit home or I would have got a licking for my pains. But the sport was grand in the cold weather, and much better than lying about the house. I was now begining to get tired of books and school and often used to envy both of them [the Kinnear brothers] when I would be learning my lessons at night and heard their laughter outside playing with the rest, for none of them at this place went [to school] but my self. So when summer came on I got my father to let me work a half drill at the turnip thinning, and all harvest, promising to go back to school in winter. Which I did, and got on much better for my holiday.

My father was anxious to do something for me, as I was the youngest and he had more to give me than the rest. But I was more inclined to follow the plough and was very fond of horses. Besides, I could not think of any life that was as far from care as a ploughman. So I would not set my mind on any other trade but just let me be like my father – an honest ploughman. For had I not often heard him say that, take him all in all, the ploughman was as well paid at the year's end as the tradesman, and in bad times far better?

Well, my father resolved to leave here, as my brother James had taken to poaching along with the young master. And, as my father was against night work of any kind, he went off to Dalkieth, to the fair, and met in with Mr Wight, his former master, who was looking for a grieve. Although my father was still against going east to Berwickshire, still he [Wright] would not take a denial, telling him he would be much better off than at House of Muir and offering more wages, which tempted my father to accept. So we left the only place I was ever sorrow to leave, [and be] apart from the play mates I was never to see for many long years.

We arrived at Ecclaw, in the month of May 1868. I may say that if I was sorrow to leave our old place, I was as grieved to come here where there was nothing to view but whins and heather and bleak mountains. There was nothing to attract my attention but the sea, which I had never seen before but only from the top of the Moorfoot Hills where we used to get a view of the Firth of Forth. But here was a mighty ocean with a coast line as far as the eye could reach, and streaching away to the horizon where the sea and sky seemed to blend together till you could not tell which was which. If it had not been for my old school mate at Pathhead, Bill Wight [...]

Bill took me on long rambles over the hills to the various trout streams to fish. And [we] went hunting with the dogs in the dean which ran right through the farm and was a veritable rabbit warren. Or often times [we would go] rambling down one of the smaller trout streams till we arrived at the sea, where we used to explore the rocks and crevices from the Peas Sands. [This was] a lovely streach of sand. The only place where the might[y] breakers could roll themselves [in]to the tinyes and wains that ripples until you could hardly imagine the same power [it was] which heaved the huge mountain of waves which broke with unceasing roars and monotonus regularity from St Abb's Head to Thornton Lough [Thornton Loch, East Lothian].[15] With this one exception [they] were part and parcel of the same might[y] ocean and heaved from the same bosom. Until we'd reach the cave or fishermen's harbour where we used to get grand fun with the fisher lads and lasses – who I thought so uncouth in speach and manners at first. Bill, by this time, was great friends with them all and knew them all by name as he had been two years at school among them. Although he was a wild mischevious lad, you could not help liking him. He was very fond of the sea and the boats [and] so the fisher folks all had a work waitin [for him].

And we learned to swim that summer. At least, I did, for he could swim in a very imperfect way by this time. But I soon learned, for I was very imitative, and was not long of learning anything when once I had some one to show an example. Will, poor fellow, was to nead his swimming lessons one day not far distant, for his father sent him off to sea the following year – apprentised for seven years to an East Indian merchant man, and he never saw him again.

By and by I got used to our new quarters, although I never learned to reconcile my self to them, and after a few weeks I got on to groom the ponies as the groom ran away. As it was arranged by my father and the master, I was to get my meals in the big house with a fee at the half-year's end. I only went home to sleep. Here I had little time to myself. Having to rise at half past four in the morning, be in the stable at five, groom a pair of ponies and be in the field at six with the women – and keep up my drill at the turnips, singling or hoeing. [Then] sort the ponies at dinner time and clean any dirty bits or stirrups while the rest were resting, and [then] be at the hoe all afternoon. At night I['d] often sit up till eleven or twelve o'clock waiting on the master, or his son Robert who was learning to be a farmer under his father, and then rub down the pony for half an hour [before] turning up in the morning with the rest for the hoe.

Hard lines, you will say, for a lad of twelve years. Had I been compeled to do it, most likely I would have run away like the other lad. But, you see, I was doing it of my own free will too, rather than go to school as my parents wished. So I continued at this for some time. Then, as there was some new stables and buildings in course of erection, I was set on to drive stones from a quarry down in the dean during harvest time – as all the others were engaged at the cutting. So [I] had an easier time for a week or two, till the leading-in began.

Then I was put on to take my turn with the rest. But I easily managed as the sheaves were light and, of course, I was happy if I could only get a horse to drive. So, after harvest I got turnips to drive up to Martinmas. Of course, all this time I had three horses to groom. The one I wrought with, and the two ponies. So, I rebelled and told my father I would not do it longer than the term [but] that I would like to go to Dalkieth Young Folk's Fair[16] and like to drive an odd horse[17] and learn to plough. Both my parents were against this proposal but at last yealded, thinking that a hard winter would perhaps sicken me of it and I would yet be glad to give it up and come home to school.

So, accordingly, off I went to Dalkieth Fair accompannied by my sister Jane. And we met in with our brother James in the fair – where we all hired. I to go for groom and drive the odd horse and learn to plough in the spring, my brother to drive a pair of horses, and my sister to be cook, on the neighbouring farms of Clint and Hoppringle in Gala Water near Fountainhall [Selkirkshire]. I went to Clint and my brother and sister going to Hoppringle – they going to serve with the father, I the son. Here I had to mix with a house full of strangers, which I did not like at first but soon got used to it. The only one that took kindly to me was the lass [Maggie] who was hired to look after the children. [She] was, like myself, on her trial, this being her first place. But she did not stay many weeks till she ran away home and would not come back. Her father was a shepherd on the other side of Gala, about 3 miles off. [I] often went to see her and get my tea on Sundays.

You have no conception of the life of a young lad, or lass, new from home in some of those farm houses. The quieter and better behaved you are, the more jibes and swears and cuss you get from the older ones who would always like some body on whom they could draw attention as being far worce than themselves when they were being censured for any bad behaveiour. So that you get little encouragement to behave deacently. But if you are bousterious and rude and swear at them every time you have occasion to speak, you are then considered a game one and there was something in you.

Well, we got a red-headed virago in this girl's place who kept us all in mischief and often I used to tell the other two women they ought to have been kinder to Maggie and the[y] would not have been tormented with Kate. She was about seventeen years of age and as big as any of them, and every thing [that happened] she told the mistress. Even to who came home from the church with them on Sunday. And woe betide cook an[d] [the] out-by woman had they a lad coming to see them. She would watch [the lad] away from the place, and torment [the lass] about their looks for days. How I used to hate her. And she, knowing it, returned it with interest. But I was match of her and generally, when she used to begin a racket, I used to bully her out of the face of it or trip her up and run off and laugh till she would go in the house and cus with spite. Many a row I got over it – from the master – about some paltry thing she could get to tell on me.

But enough of this, I paid her well. For the other two woman, although rough, were very kind-hearted and had none of the vindictiveness of Kate in their natures. One, the cook, was Irish – at least of Irish parentage, born in Scotland and only for her name [you would not know]. You could not tell by her tongue. The other, the out-by lass that wrought in the fields, was Scotch, and her father was a ploughman on a farm about four miles off. As she and I were companions all day mostly we got on fine, and she always carried her wallet full of bread and cheese. We got our meal in company, but of course it was only an excuse to give [the food] to me as I was always hungry long before dinner time. This was the hardest winter ever I felt or stood out in. Although a small farm – that is a small amount of arable land – there was a large amount of hill and pasture and we had to pick up turnips for the sheep, often standing up to the knees in snow. A[nd] other times, [we would be] carrying bundles of hay over the hill and on horse's back, and graiping for the sheep among the snow wreaths with pitchforks. Sometimes the men and master both would be out all night, but of course I never was taken.

Well, when the spring came on I got to plough and, although I held pretty well at first and made a fairish job, I soon tired of it. Then came the harrows which was worse, for the winter being long and severe, the work was [hard] and we had to put on all strength. So the out-by lass, Maggie Newlands, got the head

ploughman's horses to drive [and] I had to take my own pair –
the odd one, and the master's riding pony. Now, as this odd one
was the mother of all the other ones nearly, you may gues she
was pretty old and stiff. I had to keep continually flogging to
keep [her] up with the other [so] that at last I got fairly sick. I
resolved to leave off horses and take to herding till I was able
to take a pair of horses. So, on the morning of Stow Fair, on
being asked what I intended doing, I said I was going. So, of
course, I got liberty and went off with the rest, for it was to be
a clean-out. All but Ginger, the bairn-keeper, who was stopping.

So I hired to go to a shepherd to be his bondager and herd
in the summer, and feed the hogs in winter or, as then, in autumn.
So, I dissapointed my parents at home again as they fully expected I would be glad to come home from what they heard from
my brother and sister. But they never reproached me but always
wrote very kind letters to me, and my mother always wrote
reminding of my prayers night and morning. But, unless when
in any dificulty, I never prayed nor ever looked at the little Testa-
ment, that lay in the drawer of my chest, from Sunday till Sunday. I was early embarked on a road of sin, and the very fact of
having perfect freedom of action away from my parents kept me
from going back as much as anything.

Well, not long after the fair we were all sent down to Hoppringle to help with the harrowing, and of course we got our
dinner in the kitchen. Well, when we were coming away out, my
sister sliped a half bannock of peas[e] and flour (such as is used
at the master's table at dinnertime to eat to the broth) into my
pocket to eat in the afternoon, which I did. Only I had more than
I could manage, so I had this bit home with me. And in the evening, after supper, it was a customary thing for us to get milk and
bread before going to bed. So, when the milk and bannocks were
produced I minded about the bit I had left. So, I pulled it out
and began to eat it to my milk. So, when Ann, the cook, saw me,
she say, 'Surely you think far more of your own sister's baking
than you do of mine that you carry them (meaning the bannocks)

up here to eat it?' Instead of trying to conciliate her, as I might have done, I say to her, 'These are far better than you bake.' So up she got and tells the mistress who came ben and asked me if I had any faults with the bread I got. 'None ma'am. If any other person in the house can eat them, I can. If you always give me plenty, I care nothing about the quality.' How did I notice to tell cook that the others are better? 'So they are', says I. 'And better than any ever I got since I came here.' So she flew in a great rage, an ben to the master, who came to see all about it. So, I lifted a bit of the bannock lying on the plate and asked him to taste it, which he did, and said he felt nothing wrong with it. 'Taste that', says I, giving him the bit in my pocket which I put in when the row began. 'Oh', says he, 'There is a great difference, but it is not in the baking.' 'I never said it was your cook'. Insisting as much, 'And I never put her off the belief she bakes very well for an Irish woman, who in the majority of cases can only cook a potatoe. She judges me by her own standard.' So the master told me to say no more about [it]. But I would not now. I said I would tell his father and mother, and my sister, the next time I saw them. I had no doubt his mother would give me a farrel up in my pocket. For his mother had more sense than either him or his braw wife, who gave us bannocks that the horses would not eat, and a dog howled on being presented with them. So, says he, 'You lie, sir. There's not a better meat house in Gala Water.' 'Yes', says I, 'In your mother's time. Or when you had a housekeeper. But I can get you plenty who will tell you a diferent story.' 'You can?' 'Yes I can. Here are three.' Here pointing to the two young chaps and my self. Says Mr Graham to one of them, 'Bob, have you any fault with the meat you get?' 'Yes', says Bob, 'An mare than me here.' The mistress' voice from the parlour cries, 'John. Come away John. Don't listen any longer to that impudent boy.' But he was not satisfied. 'So', says Maggie, the out-by woman, 'We all have reason to complain many times, but we are all going away owing to that.' The mistress [then cries], 'John, do you hear me? Come away ben. I'm wearying sitting here myself.'

So, for this row I never got pardon, and left in disgrace. And he kept the ten shillings of reference, the low, mean hound. For as hard a winter it was, [he] only gave me 2£ for six months to satisfy his own and his wife, because I told him an unpleasent truth and let them know what others cried in the market place. Well he'll yet be as hard up for ten shillings as I am. He was the only man ever said I was a bad worker and not worthy of my hire. But I also learned a lesson, which was never to trust to any man's good name for it was often very misleading. Further expeariance has taught me that the biggest rogues are the most particular of their good name, because under the protection of it they alone can carry on their deception.

Well, we all left, Ginger and all, for she got into disgrace before the term and threw-up her place. So, it was a clean sweep. So, I went to Stow, to a farm called Muirhouse, to the shepherd. His house was up on the side of the Lauder road about a mile from Stow, and about half that distance from the farm, and so was very dull. But I was seldom at home, being down at Stow every night – among the lads, or at the farm. In the shepherd's house there were nine children, some of them near as old as myself, so it was always in a muddle. You could neither read a book or write a letter for your life as there was only one end and a bit loft reached by a ladder where I had to sleep with three boys. You had to sit on the front of the bed to take off your clothes. You could not stand up in it. I often think how I stayed my time out, but I did.

I was not very well fed here, but I very often got the best in the house and I knew they had not it to give. Many a night I have gone out and caught a rabbit with my dog, on the sly, for next day's dinner, or caught a few trout in a burn about a mile distant. Well, here I got on fine outside. I got five score or so of scabbed sheep[18] to look [after], and skin an bury any that died, or killed them myself before they died. If the skin was worth takeing off I did so, if not I buried them skin and all. For this reason I was not allowed to go among the other sheep till they were all dead, for fear of infection.

Well, after the turnips were ready for singling, I had to take the hoe for the rest of the summer – which was a very hot one. The harvest coming on, I had to bind a sheaf after the machine, and hard work it was for a lad of thirteen years. But I managed pretty well, although I was often very tired at night. I stuck in [with] all my might, for I had a fine cheery lass to help who could bind a sheaf at a time when I was behind – which was not often for we were often done before some of the others who were older and stronger, as we were suppler to run between sheaves and we both liked to get a rest and a crack before the next machine came round. But this did not often occur an we were kept pretty constant at it.

Well, of course, after the cutting was over I got a horse to lead in with. But not for long, for I was set on, along with [an]-other three lads of about my size, to rake the stubble with a big rake with iron teeth, [which was] about six feet long with a leather strap for your shoulder. This we had to do for three weeks. 'Horse's work', you will say – and so it was. Up hill and down in a rough stubble field for five hours at a streatch and for twenty-one days on end. One would have been easier in the Calton[19] for the same length of time.

Well, after this was finished, I got away by myself with the sheep till Martinmas when I returned home having got a sickness at this place. Well do I remember how proud my mother was to have me home again, and how I enjoyed the tea and flour scones she pressed on me and the feeling of rest and contentment when I sank in my nice soft bed which, although only chaff, was as soft and downey as any feathers. How I thanked God, for the first time for many a day, for the blessing of such a mother and such a home.

Well, my father sent me off to school to learn Arithmetic and Drawing for the winter quarter and wanted me to stay longer. But I did not care to stay when the spring weather came in again. So I got a pair of horses to harrow and work with till the term. Well, my father took me in to Edinburgh about this time and bound me an apprentice to a friend[20] of our own, a grocer in the Cowgate. A Mr McIntosh, a cousin of my mother. Well, when

27

we had arranged all this, father took me to another friend's, a clothier and outfitter in the South Bridge, a Mr Hunter, where he got me measured for a suit of clothes to go to my new place. Now, we got into a dispute as I wanted a small waiscot without sleeves, and father, he would have one with a moleskin back a[nd] sleaves. Well, I had to give in, and he ordered what he wanted. But when we got out of the train at Cockburnspath, I spoke about it again and said it was a very unlikely thing to go stand behind a counter dressed like a ploughman. My father was angry at this and said I would have to go with it, for I would likely only run messages, or work in the cellar and clean out the shop. Well, when I heard this, I said I would not go at all, and no amount of persuasion from my mother would make me give in. As for my father, he never mentioned the subject again but kept me at home working on the farm, which I did all that summer.

About the month of July, Mr McIntosh and his sister Violet came out with his two boys, for the country air. Mr McIntosh was a widdower with four children – two girls and two boys – but his late wife's people took the girls and brought them up, as they were Roman Catholics and were afraid their aunt Violet, who was a Protestant, might use any influence over them.

So, about this time, my dear mother died, leaving us all very suddenly, but not unexpectedly. For she knew her end would come very suddenly at any time for she had a weak heart and had got a few warnings. I can remember her telling us that she would not be long with us, and asking my father to be kind to me as I was the only one she was sorrow to leave. So she just droped from her chair where she was sitting, sewing a pair of trousers for little Willie McIntosh for the Sunday, and never spoke.

Well, of course, the McIntosh's went to Edinburgh next morning and my sister Agness came down from Blackburn, where she was in service, and kept the house for us. Father was very much put about but he had a great deal of worry with the policeman about a Death Certificate which has to be produced in all cases of sudden death.[21] As he was ignorant of this it caused him a deal of unnecessary trouble which helped to keep him from brooding over his loss. As for my self, I was so stunned I could hardly realise what had occurred.

Well, my father took her remains to Cockpen [Midlothian], which was her express wish, to be laid beside that of her son Alexander, father's name son, who died before I was born. Well, we went away at two o'clock in the morning with a cart, and having got a fresh horse at Haddington [East Lothian], arrived at Cockpen about two in the afternoon, meeting all our friends and relations at Eskbank. Well do I remember how my Aunt Elizabeth, when we went into her house at Thorneybank [Thornybank] Park, Dalkieth on our journey, tired, sad and hungry, never asked us to sit down or ofered us even a cup of tea, owing to some row about my grandfather who died with us. Well, she kept up the spite against her children after she was dead. She was a hard, relentless, vindictive, selfish woman. I have thought many hard things of her since, God forgive me. However, we got home at last at one o'clock next morning and I was very tired, although I slept all the way after it turned dark and I could not see passing objects. My sister Aggie refused to come home to keep house. So, we had to write off to [my] sister Jeanie, who was in a place in Midlothian, who came home and kept house till next Whitsunday when our old home was broken-up for ever.

Well, when the hiring fair came round again, Jeanie and I went off to Dunse [Duns, Berwickshire] and I hired to Mr Johnston of Fellcleugh, over in the Lammermoor [Lammermuir] hills, about six miles from home as the crow flies. (I may state, before going further, that my brother Stephen had come home from the army after serving his term of ten years and had been at home for nearly a year, so that there was only three at home now – father, Stephen and Jeanie. Agness was still at service and Mary, George and James were married and had homes of their own.[22])

Well, I liked this place very much. I was well done to have a very kind master, and his sister – who kept house for him – was a particularly nice woman and took a great interest in the young folks. Although she was on the high side of forty, she considered herself quite young and liked nothing better than to get a dance in the kitchen among the rest, more especially if a certain young ploughman who had a sneaking fondness about her, went ben for her.

Well, about the New Year my sister, Jeanie, got married to a certain David Kinnear – a brother of my old playmates at Outerstone [Outerston], but some years older. I mind fine that night they were married. I asked away in the old year's night to be at the wedding, but as some of the others were going away also I had to stay and do my usual work before I could go. By which time it was dark, and I was nervous in the dark myself and having six miles over the moor through bogs, burns and scaurs[23] [to travel]. Well, off I started at last, about five o'clock and very dark, and took three miles of moor without a tract of any kind to guide me. But, by dint of caution and taking my bearings from the position of the hill tops, I found the road in safety after nothing worse than a tumble up against a wire fence and another into a sheep drain.

When I got on the road I thought I was all right and was spanking along as fast as I could travel when lo, I ran up against something in my hurry which made my hair stand on end. But what it was I could not make out at the time. But after it had surveyed me for a few moments, it quietly walked away and left me speachless and motionless. For if I had had the power of speach I would have cried [out], not being far from the farm of Bowshielhill [Berwickshire]. [In truth] all that I had seen was the Laird's tame deer which had broken out of its park. Well, after coming to a bit, I started off to the houses to tell what I had seen, firmly believeing I had seen the Devil. But after I had reflected a bit, I just passed by and never let on, as I thought they would only laugh at me for my pains. So I passed quietly by and down the brae and through the burn, climbing across on a water gate and up the brae on the other side past Nether Monynut, where I breathed freer after I got rid of the dark shaddows of the glen [and got] on to the hill top.

So, [I] was begining to get over my fright [when] I heard the fearfullest noise ever I had heard – right up over my head. So thinks I, here he is again and so I'll go back to Monynut and see if any person will see me over the hill. But again the fearfull buzzing started, this time so near that I was quite frightened out of my witts and ran off home like mad. Well, I had to run over a bridge, over a small brook, futher on. But no bridge could I see and [so] just took it at the nearest, up to the knees. But I never slacked speed till I was a mile further on, overlooking the stream and moor, where I stoped for want of breath. [I] was walking on as fast as my shaking legs would carry me when I heard the same cry again, rather before me this time. So off I started again down the hill past the star like any […] running a muck, till I arrived at the moor where I was very well acquainted with the farmer. But I was in the kitchen some time before I could tell what was wrong with me. So, he said he would see me over into sight of Ecclaw. So, after he was out on the road a bit I drew his attention to the noise further up the hill where I had first heard. 'Oh' says he, 'I kenned what it was fine when ever I heard your description. You'll get acquainted wie that gin ye bide lang in the hills. It's just the snipes taking a bit dive to themselves.'

Well to make a long story short, after I parted with the man and the moor, I soon reached home where I got a hearty welcome. For the marriage having been performed, the supper was in full swing so I was soon happy and forgot all about my fright and never told anyone about it till next day, when I told Stephen. He got a fine laugh at my expense.

So my favourit sister being married, and my other one refusing to come home and keep house, my father broke up his home and went away to single service away up in Ettrickdale. Stephen got on to the railway for a surfaceman[24] near Tynehead [Midlothian] on the Hawick and Carlisle route of the NBR [North British Railway].

I went off home to my place on the morrow and stayed up till Whitsunday, when I went off with the shepherd to Mr Johnston's brother, who had taken the farm of Kidshielhaugh [Berwickshire], about four miles from Duns. He was an old shepherd who had been in Ireland for twenty years and had made as much money as take a farm at home. He went off to Ireland whenever he was married, so all his family were born in that country and they were proud of it. They were allways ready to stick up for Old Ireland and you could not do them a worse turn than say they were Scotch-Irish.

Their mother was supposed to be the bonniest lassie in the Lammermuirs and I could well believe it for she was still a very good looking woman of middle age – say between forty and fifty years. She had seven a[s] fine looking daughters as you could find in Scotland. But their love of things Irish led one of them into a sad mistake. Ann, the second oldest, was betrayed by an Irishman who came to harvest with her father and who turned out to have a wife at home, and three children. Poor girl. I was sorrow when I heard of it, for she was the favourit of the lot.

Well, here I was up in the hill again, our house being about a mile up in the hill – as the most of the shepherds houses are so that they can be nearer to gather the flock in stormy weather. Well, I got on pretty well, although I was very much disapointed in my master who I thought a nice man when I neighboured[25] him at Felcleugh [Fellcleugh]. But I soon found out that those who were your best friends when they had no power over you, soon changed when they got it. Well, I have found it so, since he was very harsh to me and once chased me with a pitchfork for something I had said to him. For I would not recognise his authority when I was working along with the rest of the workers, but only when I was sent with him, by the master, among the sheep, when he would be as pleasant a[s] you could wish. 'Twas only among the others he was dogmatic, but I was more than a match for him untill he was forced to give it up. [He] was very anxious for me to stop [with him], as I often went round the hill for him in the Sabbath morning (when he was in his bed or when he went to church), and often in the mornings before going to a hard day's work, but I would not stay.

I had [nae] liking for strange scenes and strange faces and I was anxious to get back to the Lothians again where I had some friends. For here all were strangers, cursing all the time. I never was inside of a church door, nor had I ever a visit of a minister. On Sundays I wandered at my own sweet will over the hill away up by Longformacus [Berwickshire], and even as far as the top of Dirrington Laws. There are two Laws, both of a size and both riseing out of the level plain far above the neigbouring hills here. You are well rewarded for your hard climb, for you have spread out before you the mural of Berwickshire from Duns to Berwick-on-Tweed and far away over the Scottish border into Northumberland. In fact, you have the whole of the fertile valley of the Tweed, from Kelso to Berwick, with the Cheviots looming in the distance. Often, as I have sat up here and read a book or ate my bit of bread and cheese, the sun shining on the distant border fortresses crumbling with age, I have thought no wonder our forefathers strove for their homes. For here was a land worthy of their best efforts to retain, flowing with milk and honey.

At other times I was wont to picture to myself the battles and forrays which had been fought out on that same scein of hill and dale in the days of yore, where right was might and when the guid wife dished up a pair of spurs to her guid man's dinner as a sign that the larder was nearly empty.

At other times I used to go up on the Cockburn Law [Berwickshire], and here you had much the same view, only you could see much further toward the sea. You had the village of Abb[e]y St Bathans [Berwickshire] on the north side of you nestling among the trees with, here and there, a glint of the river Whiteadder as it glided slowly along. This was my favourit walk, and after going up on the laws I went down to the village then walked down the river side for about two miles to a place called Cockburn Mill [Berwickshire]. Going back home up the other side of the law, I remember there was an old castle[26] on the hill-side overlooking the river, with a few goosberries bushes inside of the walls. Here, I spent a whole Sunday afternoon with some more lads about my own age who knew about them formerly. After filling our bellies and pockets, we began throwing them at

33

one another till darkness overtook us [and] we had to proceed home in the dark.

Once, I got a very unpleasent surprise when the post man called and told me there was a letter at Duns for me containing money, and that I would have to go to Duns for it myself [as] there was something to pay for it. So off I went, four miles on a dark night on a road I had only traveled twice before. After going to the Post Office and paying for my letter and coming out side, I opened the envelope with trembling fingers for I fully expected something great. When, lo and behold, out pops a six penny piece, for which I had paid eightpence – double registration fee. Well, I took it to the post master and explained that my sister sent it me and that it was very hard for me to pay so much. But he ordered me out. And, says he, 'Perhaps that will learn your sister not to try and defraud the Post Office again.' 'Well' says I, 'You should have made my sister pay the piper and not me'. Well, I returned home in great rage without reading my sister's letter and I fully intended to write her a sharp letter in return. But on reaching home, and before going to bed, I lighted my candle and read my letter and so [learned] this was a sixpence to post a letter with. Dear Jeanie, if she had only known what trouble and expense it would cost me she would never have sent [it]. I knew [this], so after reading her very kind letter with good advise and kind wishes I was quite pleased, and when I wrote I never mentioned it for fear of vexing her, but just thanked her for it, saying I had got it all right.

Well, I would not stay any longer than the term, when I parted good friends with all my mates and I never saw one of them since. There was one I was often going back to see but I never got the length [of it] – through force of circumstances more than want of will. For I was not hired for the next half year, and had never the money to pay a railway fare.

I went and stayed with my sister Jane at Carlaverock [Farm], a place near Tranent, where I got some work on the farm. But the winter proved a hard one, and when the snow storms came there was no work. So I went off to my other sister, Mary, who was married to a policeman in Selkirkshire called Roderick McLean. Here I stayed for three weeks, tramping through the hills with him, going his daily rounds. I enjoyed it very much, although [the hills] were all covered with snow, knee-deep.

Well, my sister soon packed me off as she said I was learning her little boy, a boy of two years, to speak like an Irish man. I was very fond of speaking Irish, having got the twang from the Johnstons in Berwickshire who – as I have told you – were fond of the Irish and spoke the brogue beautifully. Well, after leaving Borthwick Bank, for that was the name of the place (the Police Station was called Roberton [Selkirkshire]), I came to Dalhousie Mains [Midlothian], where my brother James was a ploughman. I got a job at Newbattle Brick Works. But as I only got a lad's pay and had to work a man's work, wheeling heavy barrows of brick, I resolved to leave as soon as possible and getting a chance I left in three weeks.

Well, I got to work with a gardiner at a small house on the roadside between Cockpen Manse and Bonyrigg [Bonnyrigg, Midlothian], which had been left as a legacy to Mr Merricks of Roslin Powder Mills.[27] [He] had the grounds all laid out in walks and planted with trees by a gardiner from Edinburgh with whome I wrought till the job was done, when he [then] recommended me to the mason who came to sort up the house.

So I got work till May, the easiest work ever I was at. This mason was Mr Merricks over-man from the mills, on days wages. So you were not hard wrought. To me, who had been used [to] toiling to a farmer, it was liker play than work. Only some times you had [to strive], when the stones were to [be carried] up the gangway. But not often, for we had not much building [and] mostly [it was] repairs – picking out mortar from between the stones so that the masons could give her a point over outside to make her new again. After that was done, I was set on to polish up a stone for a headstone to the late lamented owner of the house – which took a long time and which I was heartily sick of. But I could not get on, for the mason who had the job used to make me take a smoke every half hour. Often I have seen him empty out the good drinking water I had brought not long before and send me off to the manse for more, and tell me to take a good long crack with the maid and not come back till dinner time. This man ha[d] started as a builder in Roslin some years ago and has a lot of property. Mr Merricks failed in the powder mills, which are now the property of a London firm, with Mr Merricks as manager.

Well, at Whitsunday my brother flitted away from Dalhousie Mains and so I went back to Carlaverock [East Lothian] for a few days. As there was no work to be got I went off to Dunbar Runaway Fair[28] with my bundle under my arm. Meeting in with Mr Wight of Ecclaw, [I] hired to him and went home in his gig at night with him. Well, I got my old job, to be groom and work with the women only. I had only one pony to sort, and to drive out and in the cows morning and night. I fell in to my old groove and got on fine. The people about the place were all new since I had left, but I soon got acquainted with them all as I was beginning to have more cheek among strangers.

The cook was the only one who knew me when I went back as she was an out-by worker under my father, and she was very kind to me. There was a young girl about my age in the house and she appropriated me at once for her lad. Now, had it come off my side it would have been all right. But when she took possesion of me as it were, I was furious for I was very bashfull, and cared nothing for a lass.

Often, when I was reading in the kitchen at night, or a Sunday afternoon, she would come and sit down beside me and try to draw me into a conversation about what I was reading. Had we bean ourselves I would have done nicely, but cook, who saw that I was bashfull, used to say what a nice looking pair we made. Of course, this made me worse and often I rose and went away out on one pretence or another, just to get out of banter. Well, of course, the girl turned. She would not come near me or speak to me if she could help. In course of time we came to be foes. [It was] the only time ever I willingly made any girl unhappy, for I did torment her awfully, although I had a likeing for her through it all.

Well, harvest came on after a very warm summer and we were at the leading-in of the corn. I took ill of a feaver which kept me in bed for two months, during which time I had to be removed to the farm house as the doctor would not allow me to be kept in the stable loft. Well, here I made an enemy of the mistress. For after all her kindness, I would not allow her to look into the garret where I lay. When ever I heard her tougue I would commence to curse at her fearfully. For although I was delerious for the first six weeks, still her voice would irritate me, even when she was asking for me at the bottom of the stair. She being of a very unforgiving spirit, she kept it up against me, and asked me several times after I was up, what ever she had done that I hated her so? [She] gave me a good [be]rateing for my ingratitude etc. which I had just to bear in silence as I could not give an explaination of my dislike and only said that, being unconcious, I was not responsible for my actions and people often did very odd thing[s] in the hight of feaver.

But she never was the same to me after and told me that I brought the feaver into her house – although her own daughter took it the very day I did. We both took to bed at the same time. Then Mr Wight took it a month later, but he never rose again. He died shortly after. I left at Martinmas when I was able. I [had] started to turnip driveing and continued for a week or two when I had a row with old Mrs Wight over a very trifling affair. But any thing was good enough for an excuse to vent her splean on me now I was going away. This particular night I was late, wet and hungry and, of course, angry [and] I had to wait a long time [for] the housemaid, the girl I told you before whose friendship I rejected. As soon as she came and gave me my porridge she whipped up the small lamp that stood on the kitchen table and went away leaving me in the dark, for there was a close[d] range and [it] gave no light. Well, when she had brought it back, I said she might light a candle when she went into the back kitchen. She gave me a very sharp answer about minding my own busness and in a few minutes returned to take the lamp again. But I put out my hand and said I would not take my supper in the dark to please her as I did not think it was intended I should. So, in the scuffle for possesion of the lamp we broke it and they in the parlour, hearing the noise of the breaking glass, came running to see what it was. The girl said I did it, and I that she did, and gave my reason for wishing to retain it. Mrs Wight was speachless with rage but her daughter comenced the onslaught on me like any gipsy tinker, till she was out of word and breath. So, I told her she could keep her tinker jaw to herself as I did not mind it, being pretty well used to it now. And, as she was neither master or mistress, she had nothing to do with [it]. If she had not been an impudent hussy, she would not have interfeared. So, not having recovered her breath, she ran off to the parlour and cried for an hour. Well, now that the field was left to herself, the old lady commenced to upbraid me for my behaiour to her daughter. I listened patiently till she was done. Nor was it my intention to speak back, as she was an old woman and I only a lad. Had she been content to lash me, but she went on to say it was ill of my part to be so rude to Miss Wight after all she had done for myself and our family. Well this riled me up again and I said she was an old hag, and fifty other not very handsome names. She never did anything for me but gave me her worst word whenever she got an opportunity. As for doing anything for our family, both my parents had done for herself and family what money would not repay. I could tell her a few of these if she liked, but she went off in high dudgeon ben beside her daughter.

On coming into the kitchen that night, after this row, it was amusing to see the airs of both. Whenever I looked at them they sniffed their noses in the air like a war horse smelling the battle from afar. In the morning I got orders from the steward that I was to see the Mrs before I yolked.[29] After sorting the horses I went in to get my breakfast as usual, but was told by the cook I was to get none till the mistress came down. So I told her to go tell the Mrs I was wateing on her. So she did, and brought down word she would be down at eight o'clock. So, I wated as patiently as I could till she came down, when she told me that after considering all night she would forgive me on condition I would beg Miss Wight's pardon for what I had said to her. But I told her I was not sorrowed for what I had said as I considered she had no business with me whatever, and so I would see her far enough. First, this brought on another outburst of temper and she ordered me off the place. So, I said I would be proud and happy to go on condition I got my lying wages. She screamed, 'You'll get no wages till the term.' 'Give me my breakfast then and I'll go to my work till that time.' 'You'll get no breakfast here, nor money either. Go about your business.' The old vixen turned me off without money or breakfast, and well knowing I had no home to go to. So, off I went as I stood. I left my box in the stable. Her son Robert, who was master outside, was standing in [the] engine house door as I passed, but we never spoke. So, I traveled that day to Tranent, and all I got on the way was a Sweadish turnip out of a field at Beltonford [East Lothian].

So I stayed with my sister Jane till the term and went off back to Cockburnspath, with the train and up to Mrs Wight. 'What do you want here?' said she on my arrivle. 'My wages.' 'Where have you been?' 'About my business, where you sent [me].' 'Have you seen your father?' 'No.' 'Did you write to him?' 'Yes.' 'And what did he say?' 'Nothing I was to repeat to you.' 'You're an impudent fellow.' 'I know, and mean to be, but you can't keep [from] being if you tried.' 'I'll not give you your wages unless you beg Miss Wight's pardon,' says she. 'You can go to h___ [hell], you and Miss Wight both. And perhaps you'll not be so fond of people begging your pardon when you come back. I did not come here to beg or bow to either of you, but only to ask my money which you will be in unlawfull possesion of after this date. So, if you say before those preasent I am not to get it, I'm off again.' 'Wait till I see Robert' says she. 'Kirsty gang out for the master and tell him I want him.' So when he came he says, quite free like, 'Hullow Andrew. Where have you been and what took you away without coming to me first?' 'Because I knew you had no say in the matter and were only master as long as you said with your mother, like your father before you. If you were master, why did you not take [them] in hand before? Do you think I was wrong to rebell against sitting at my meals in the dark like a dog?' 'No, I didn't, and I told my mother so. But you broke the lamp and gave my mother and sister ill temper, when, if you had come to me, or spoken to my mother quietly, we would have put that right.' 'Yet your sister gave me more ill tongue than ever I got from the worst rowdy ever I came across. And your mother wanted me to go on my knees to her. Well, I will not go over the same ground again. Give me the wages and I'll clear out. You'll be glad to get rid of me.' So the old mistress asked him if I was to get my wages and he said he didna ken. So she told me to wate a minute and she would soon be back. So, when she came back carying my wages she wanted me to go and pay the doctor for his attendence when I was ill and bring her the receipt. But I said, no, I would pay the doctor as I went home, but all that was my business not hers. So she gave me 5£, and I told her she had surely forgot herself as I had got 10s during the summer. Well, after she went back and changed the [money] to give me the 4£ 10s she came back, quite pleased that [I] had not taken the advantage, and asked me if I had got any meat since I came, and would have taken me ben to dinner with them in the parlour. I said, no, but I would rather beg than eat in her house, and came off out of the house and never said 'Thanks' or 'Good Day' to any of them.

When I was going out of the door, Robert, who was in the back kitchen, said that was a bad spirit I had, and he was afraid I would not get very well through the world with […]. So, I told him, if God granted me health and strength, I would get through the world when he would starve. So, that was the last I saw of any of them for many a year after this.

My father took up house again, getting my sister Agness to come home and keep it for him at a place called Fushie Bridge, [Midlothian]. Here we stay[ed] for six months. My brother, Stephen, working on the railway, and my father getting work cutting wood at Vogrie. So, I went on trieing and got a job on the railway works near Pennicuik [Penicuik, Midlothian] where there was a small branch line making here. I got on fine with the navies till the frost set in, when we were knocked up. So, I went and got a start beside my father at the wood, to drive a horse and draw the trees into lotts after they were cut and primed. We had to walk four miles, night and morning, in snow up to the knees – but we got work for two months, when all [other] outside work was at a stand. We were very glad of it when we got open weather again. This job being done, I got on at Arniston Brickwork [Midlothian] but, as I was still a lad, it was hard work. I wrought two month for under pay[30], during which time I was working a full man's work. So, I asked my pay up, but the foreman would not grant it. So [I] gave in my warning and left. I got a few weeks work driving lime stone at Caperstone Lime Works and left at the term, having been in four places in six months.

My father and Stephen having hired to go back to Mr Stenhouse (their old master) at Dalkieth Fair, we all flitted to Gyle, South Gyle [Edinburgh, Midlothian].[31] As I had not been hired, it was my intention to go into Edinburgh to try my luck, after I saw them flitted. But one of Mr Stenhouse's men left at the term – some row about horses – and my father got me to take them. I got to drive dung from Edinburgh, two rake per day. Harid, dirty work, but I liked it as I saw a little more of life than working on the farm constantly.

Well, I stayed on at this till after harvest time, and having been sent to drive potatoes from a neighbouring farm – some which Mr Stenhouse had bought at a roup – I had a row with my father and left him the horses standing on the field and went off to Edinburgh. From there I walked to Blackshiels Mains [Midlothian] – commonley called Frosty Neb – where my brother, James, was. Well, I stayed all night with them and started for Tranent to Jeanie's, where I always went when there was anything wrong with me. Here I got a job from Mr Stobo to work at potatoe lifting for a few weeks, during which time I got intimation of a job in Leith Walk [Leith, Midlothian] to drive a wood cart with Mr [...] Mitchell at the sawing and moulding mill at 19s per week, which I gladly accepted.

Before I was three weeks there I got an advance of one shilling per week owing to a strike amoung the lorry men and carters. Although we made no agitation for an advance, we got the shilling of advance whenever it was conceded by the larger contractors. Well, here I had a pound per week. Had I been a saving lad, I might have put away a good few pounds in the bank which would have been of advantage to me in after years. But I got in among a very drunken lot of men, and into a bad set at my lodgeings. I soon got to be as bad as any and turned fond of the whisky, and was often wating till the shops opened in the morning to get one to put me right.

I went to lodge with my cousin, Andrew Ramage, who had been over twenty years at the woodcutting and was a drunken neer-do-well who never had a suit but the one he wore at work. I was soon in the same position and could hardly appear respectable at my work, far less get a suit for Sunday, and was only once inside of a church all the time I remained in Edinburgh.

Well, to go back to the time I left my father, who, when I left him in the field, thought I was away home to the house. But what was his astonishment on coming home to learn that I had never gone home. He concluded I had gone to the Castle[32] to list as I [had] often spoke of doing. Well, my sister Agness and another girl went about the roads nearly all night looking for my return. And Aggie went to Edinburgh next day and visited the castle and Piershill Barricks [Edinburgh], but no Andrew [was] to be found, so she had to go off home disconsolate. Nor did she stay long after before she also left and went to a place in Edinburgh.

So my brother, Stephen, who was now the only one left at home, had to take to himself a wife for the sake of a housekeeper. He got married about the month of April to a Bewickshire woman. I was his best man at the wedding, which was a very quiet one owing to a death in the family which was caused by small pox, which was then making ravages all over the country and especially in the towns – being very bad in Leith where I was resideing.[33]

Well, I stayed six months with Mr Mitchell and I liked the

work very well but I left owing to a few words he had occasion to speak to me for some fault. But at this time I was very biggoted in my self and would not give in, even when I knew, on reflection, I was wrong. So I wrought my warning and got a start at the Burgh Saw Mills[34], Bonnington Road [Edinburgh] with a Mr William Stewart at the same work – only we had a deal green wood[35] to drive from the country, which was rough rugged work and at which I had some very narrow escapes.

There was a new Cala railway[36] making from Slateford to Balerano [Balerno] and we had all the wood which came off it as [the track] skirted the Water of Leith all the way up. The trees, after being felled, had to be drawn up on to the road above by means of block and tackle, for it was impossible to take a horse or cart down. You could hardly climb down yourself holding on by the undergrowth. You may imagine it was a very tough job to set up trees varying from two to three tons. I have seen three cart and five men, and the master, leaving Leith at 5.30 a.m. and after getting up and loading three trees, not get back till 2.00 a.m. next day. If we got home at 10.00 p.m. same day we left, we were well pleased with our day's performance. As I was the youngest and best used at this kind of work, I got all the climbing down to adjust the tackle to do.

As we were allowed nothing but drink I have often been so d_k [drunk] I have fallen down to the water's edge amid the laughter of the others. I, of course, liked to take my glass with the others and as I was young and not so well seasoned, this was a frequent occurrence. I have often been so sore next day I could hardly walk, but of course I got fly and, as my horse was strongest and mostly set to draw the tackle, I stuck to him and let some of the others take their turn. Once we were sent over to Aberdour [Fife] to load a lighter in the harbour – which was the worst job ever I got. Once, while taking down a large plain tree which weighted twelve tons, I was nearly run into the sea as we had to come down a very steep incline between a wall from the village to the shore. Here I was terribly afraid, for although I did not know exactly the weight of the load, I also knew, by the way the horses were working, it was very heavy. So, I told Mr Stewart I would not take it down on wheels as the horse would not be able to controle it. So he brought forward the next load, took the janker off, [and] chained it to the back of the one I had. So, trailing four tons on the road, we proceeded down the hill, the horse having as little controle over the load [as] I would have had. So, when we reached the bottom of the lane I made every exertion by word and rein to stop him, and only succeeded when his fore feet was over the sea brae head, by quiting his head and running back and throwing a bang stick in front of the janker wheel. The jerk, caused by the stick under the wheel, broke the chain and so dropped the tree on the ground. Otherwise the horse would have been done for. Well, when we had extricated the poor beast from his perilouse position and relifted our loads and got safely to the pier head, we found our trouble had been in vain as the crane would not lift it. So, we had to cut it to get it on board.

We had some fine fun here at night. We all got our meals in the inn where our horses stood, but had to lodge in a labourer's home on the outskirts of the village. Some of the others soon found out that he liked his dram and they filled him d_k [drunk] a time or two so [they] got the house to themselves to hold high carnival in with his wife and daughters (he had two).

I was the musecian, with a Jew's harp I always carried in my pocket. Twice we carried on all night till morning, till some complained to the guid wife. So, after [that] we were shanked off upstairs to the bedroom at ten.

Well, soon after this I left as I was anxious to get a [horse-drawn] lorry to drive as I knew several lorrymen who, like myself, came from the country and were always telling me what a good job it was. So, I got a start with Messrs Worsley & Co at Leith north, but I did not think much of it after I got in, driving out of the docks to the station the whole day or from the station to the malt barns. What made me like it worse, I got an old horse with a greasy leg which I had to wash with black soap[37] and paint with blue stone[38] every night – often after all the rest were away home. Sometimes I had fine fun, when I was in the humour to enjoy it. When I was at the blueston[e] butt[e]ring on, I had to stand in the next stall and slash it on with a piece of tow tied on a long stick. You should have [seen] his heals flying when ever he saw it coming. It would have made a cudday [cuddy] laugh.

Our stableman and gaffer was not a good man. For if you did not feed him with drink he would give you all the dirty jobs to do, while if you stood him a drink you got all the best. So, as I would not drink with him, or even take one from him, he kept me continually driving in the docks. I don't ever remember of getting a turn up to the town all the time [I was there]. However, I got a new horse from Stirling and, as he kicked very bad when the shafts rubbed his legs, I was set on to drive to Taylor & Co from South Leith to Musselburgh [East Lothian] – two rake being a day's work. Well, this was a very good day's work and little work to do. I could have been home at five o'clock every night, but I timed myself to the right time for fear of any complaint or perhaps getting some other runs. I remember one night I was in good time. Mr Taylor's foreman had word away to the station for a lorry to deliver a load of scrap in the docks and no word of it coming. And, of course, you won't get in to the docks after six o'clock without [it having] some special arrangement [so] he asked me if I would do it on the quiet. He would give me half a crown, and so I agreed to go. After I agreed to go, and after I got on fifteen boxes of scrap to be delivered to twelve different ships, off I started and took two hours to do it as some of the ships, lying in the middle of the docks, had to send a boat to take me off and set me ashore again. Well, I had to get the money for each lot, and I got something to myself and a horn of grog which had me fairly d_k [drunk] by the time I had got them all away. Well, when I got up to the stables I was useless, and just took off the horse's harness and went off home to my lodgings. Well, next night the gaffer asked where I had been last night, I was so long. So, I said I had a lot of extra work to do at Taylors. So, he asked what it was. So, I said I had mixed loads

45

which took a long time to load and disload. But I saw he did not believe me as some of his croonies [cronies] had told him I was in the Albert dock. So, he set the clerk from the office at me and I told him what I was doing and said I did not think, when the lorry was paid for by the day, he had any business to ask an account of me for my day's work. Nor has he, said he, but perhaps some of the men lost a tip and so set him on [me]. Well, after this he never spoke to me unless it was an order. But I was not long in getting my gong[39] as the lorrymen were aggitating for two shillings more per week.

Well, to make a long story short, it was resolved at a meeting in Edinburgh that if the [masters] did not conceed the advance, we would all turn out at the foot of Leith Walk and march in process in to Edinburgh, there to make a demonstration.

Well, the masters conceeded the rise but the delegates never sent word to Leith, but left us to learn it as best we could. So, we turned out and marched up the Walk to find the Edinburgh men all working. So we returned as speedily as possible only to find a good few of us were not required, as strays from the docks had away our horses. Well, I was one and so I just did the next best thing I could under the circumstances. As the stray had taken my work, I just turned stray porter in the docks for the next three weeks till I heard of an opening with Messrs Howie & Co[40] at the Waverley, where I stayed a good long time.

Here, I may say, I drank worse than ever for there was always plenty to be got gratis at the breweries and distilleries and bonds.[41] Here I might have made money, if I had been so inclined, for I was well liked by all the merchants and others where I went for orders. As I was always very obliging, I got many a tip. I used to reckon on four shillings per day for tips, and my drink at the breweries. Then, of course, I had the tips for night.

As the most of us in the stable where my horse stood were young unmarried men, we seldome went home till we were put out of the public house where we had some queer ogries, about which the less said the better. I was with Messrs Howie & Co about a year, during which time I was in three different lodgings.

I was first lodged with a Mr George Dickson in Leith Walk. His house and shop was situated at the entrance gate to Tod[d] & Co Engineers Works and he kept a sheebeen on Sunday which never was caught. Although it was well watched by the detectives, they always came at the wrong time. Old George was always in bed ill and when ever he got the hint from his daughter, who kept the front shop and sold sweeties and lemonade, he whipped the Greybeard[42] under the blankets. Of course it never was looked for there.

Well, my father and Stephen advised me to leave this shop. So, I agreed to go and lodge with Stephen at a place called Damhead, near Gorgie [Edinburgh]. So, I stayed with him from before the new year till Whitsunday, when he flitted. I was very glad. For although I liked Stephen's wife as a landlady very well, I did not like to be so far from the stables. It was too far to walk in the mornings. I could get a car[43] to Coltbridge [Edinburgh] at night but had to walk in the morning. So, after my brother flitted to Southfield, near Portobello, [Midlothian] I took lodgeing with one of my mates who lived in Little Lochend Close, Cannon Gate [Canongate, Edinburgh]. The back entrance was oposite Jacob's Ladder [Edinburgh] and very quiet, but the front entrance is the roughest and noisiest in Edinburgh. But I was nearer my work and could get in to all my meals, which was a great blessing. And I could stay out or come in at night when I liked. Whereas, when I was late at Damhead[44] I got a lecture. There were [an]other three carters lodged here and few nights but we had a lowse and a song or two and were altogether a happy family. The landlady was a West Calder [West Lothian] woman and many a yarn I got from her about her young days in the country when she was in farm service, and we got on fine together. So I stayed with her till I left to go to the harvest, when I went off on tramp along with Sandy Kinnear out to Lauderdale [Berwickshire].

We tramped all the way seeking work. We had one or two adventures on the way. We had plenty of cash, so we made ourselves quite happy and dined and drank sumptuously. By the way, I remember when we were going up by Blackshiels [Mid-lothian], and amusing ourselves by jumping over the pailing on the road side. Our antics drew the attention of two young women who were engaged leading hay in a haugh down at the water side below. So, they got their little shoulder shawls stuck up on the pitchforks they were using, and waving them in the air drew our attention. So, off we set down the hill till we arrived at the two blooming haymakers and such a jolly afternoon we had. We got a spare rake the piece and fell to, and wrought like bricks for about an hour and a half, till it was all done. Then we lay down among the hay and the girls fished out some bread and cheese and we had the whisky after getting them to crie. But, of course, it was only pretence on their part. We fell to the bread and cheese and had a hearty meal. So, after getting a song from both, and a promise to meet some other day if we liked to come, we parted at half past five p.m. and trudged on over Soutra Hill [Midlothian], and passing Channel Kirk [Channelkirk, Berwick-shire] and Oxton [Berwickshire] arrived at Lyleston farm, foot sore and leg wearied only to find we were ...

DIARY

Part I
(1888–1889)

Andrew's sons, Duncan (Dow), Alexander (Sandy)
and George (Dod), *c*.1888.

Sunday November 1888

THIS day I have been at the church where the sacrament of the Lord's Supper was dispensed by Mr Marjoribanks, who I firmly believe to be an earnest minister of the Gospel and humble follower of our dear Lord. Whatever others may think, I for one would be ill to convince to the contrary, who [...] has seen him with tears in his eyes and his voice choked with emotion, exhorting all to come forward to the table of the Lord. Not only members of this congregation but any others preasent, whatever their creed or whatever denomination, for now was their opportunity. If, behind yon tears an[d] evident emotion, he hides an athiest's laugh as some would have us believe, then I say, may God have mercy on his soul and awake him to the knowledge that he sleepeth on the very brink of the most horrible of pits and eateth and drinketh damnation to himself, and convince him that his ministry is in vain and no good can follow or flow from it. I could not believe that he, or any man, dare to stand up and say in public that Jesus Christ our elder brother and the Son of God, never was crusified on Calvery to reaveile us to God, and yet to preach in the church him crusified and also to dispense the Lord's Supper. The idea is too revolting. They must be far gone in [guilt] and deception who could conceave it. One poor woman fainted before the service began and had to be taken outside, and another just in the middle of the sermon.

I got home at 2.45 p.m. and after dinner to a walk to Samuel's Ditch with the children, to keep them out of mischief and also to let their mother get a rest after the worry of the day. Poor soul, she has the worst of the battle.

Tuesday 20 November 1888

Snow fell heavily this forenoon and all the hill tops are covered (very cold).

Wednesday 21 November 1888

Recieved a pair of turbits from the minister of Stenton, in exchange for a pair of jacks which I sent up to him about a month ago

Thursday 22 November 1888

Another fearfull storm of wind like to blow over the old cabin. Recieved a fine CDV[45] from Mr Angus Robertson from Australia.[46] Poor chap, it's likely all ever we'll see of him, as few ever return to this country unless they prove failures out there. Got a letter from the old wife. Glad to find all in good health

Sunday 25 November 1888

Went to church with the two boys and got a very fine sermon from Mr M_ which I hope many like myself may profit by.

Tuesday 27 November 1888

Fearfull night of wind and rain. Must have been very rough at sea along the east coast. Let us hope there were few if any ships exposed to its fury.

Wednesday 28 November 1888

Grand day after the storm. No casualities as far as I have heard. Bad night last for the ploughmen attending their meeting at East Linton.

Friday 30 November 1888

Got a surprise visit from my nephew, Alexander Ramage, from Pumpherston Oil Works, Mid Calder [West Lothian], which cheered up grandfather – he not having seen [Alexander] for five years. He gave him a half sovereign on leaving.[47]

Saturday 1 December 1888

Large meeting of farm servants at East Linton to discuss the
wages question and form a union for their protection. But as
their former union was a failure so will this, as very few seems
to faviour its formation and without support it will soon die
away.[48]

Sunday 2 December 1888

Did not go to church but stayed at home to give my wife a rest
from the gate. Took a walk to Tyninghame [East Lothian] in the
afternoon. Had a discussion with some ploughmen about the
meeting held on Saturday night. All [are] against the formation
of a union or any aggitation at preasent as the country is in a
bad state, trade being very dull. I am told that Mr George Clark
of Kirklandhill was there to repudiate all conection with certain
letters in the Haddington Courrior Signed 'Farmer's Son'. Poor
chap, if he had no connection with them, his best plan was
silence. But I would be hard to convince that they did not
eminate from Kirklandhill. For all his denial, it was quite
possible his brother had a hand in them.

Monday 3 December 1888

Had a visit from my mother-in-law from Portobello. Glad to
see her looking so fresh.

Tuesday 4 December 1888

The old woman went off to Portobello today by the 11.39 a.m.
train from East Linton. Bella went to the station with her.

Wednesday 5 December 1888

Went to East Linton to enquire for a box containing three
Golden Spangle Hamburgh cock[s] which my nephew, A
Ramage, sent us a preasent from Pumpherston. Also a box
containing seven pair of trousers, one vest and two coats. Got
them home all right – with G Forsythe from Kirklandhill who
was in for coal.

Thursday 6 December 1888

Reply to A Ramage thanking him for his handsome preasents.
George at home from school with a very bad cold.

Friday 7 December 1888

Got a few lines from Rorie McLean [brother-in-law]. No news
from Comrie [sister, Agnes]. Going to send Mary Jane and Ken-
neth [the children of Rorie and sister, Mary] at the New Year
to see grandfather, God willing all the rest are in good health.
One of my young Golden Hamburgh cockirels died – the long
confinement and railway journey [had] been too much for him.
Sharp's Supper at East Linton [East Lothian].

Saturday 8 December 1888

Killed one of my best hens with a kick for ill useing the young
cock. I saw in the *Courrior* [*Haddington Courier*] about the
ploughmens' meeting at East Linton last Saturday. George Clark
seems to have been in bad breed among them. He has no call
there so it served him right, say I.

Sunday 9 December 1888

Went to church today myself, as the boys were all bad of cold.
So I got a very good sermon from one of the prophets of the
Old Testement on faith. Got home in time for the special from
B&K with the merry Andrews. Had a great meeting of plough-
men from Kirklandhill [...] all very angry at 'Farmer's Son' for
his letters in the *Courrior* [*Haddington Courier*].

Monday 10 December 1888

Had a long crack with old Bailey from Gatuide [Gateside] about
his son-in-law M McGregor. [He] has a very poor opinion of
him. Wrote a letter to Ettrick [Selkirkshire]. Weather settled and
frosty.

Wednesday 12 December 1888
Got a few lines from A Ramage. All well.

Thursday 13 December 1888
Also from A Kinnear: Do. [Ditto].

Friday 14 December 1888
Very dull foggy weather with frost in the afternoon and fresh in
the morning. Very bad for invalids. Very much troubled with my
eyes just now – too much reading papers. Must give it up for a
time, or at least read less.

Saturday 15 December 1888
Got a surprise visit from my brother, James, who came by the
nine o'clock train from Grantshouse [Berwickshire]. Was glad
to hear that all his were going about their usual business and
doing fine. He was looking very well himself, but still very much
troubled with his breath. Grandfather was very much pleased
to see him. [James] has not been for over a year and I am afraid
will not come back in a hurry.

Saturday 16 December 1888
Had a bad morning with Duncan [Dow] who was taken ill in
the morning with sickness, and vomited all over the bed. But he
got up about breakfast time and took a bit of breakfast. [He]
seemed little the worse. His uncle thought his stomach was out
of order and so we thought nothing about it, but kept him at
home from school for fear of catching cold. We got a visit in the
after noon from Agness and Ann Edmond from Oxwel[l]mains
[East Lothian]. They are looking very ill – both of them poor
girls – Ann especially. I am affraid she is far gone in consump-
tion. They had their boy, James, with them. And Duncan, he
took up at once and went out on the bank playing all the time.
They stayed about one hour. During the short time they stayed,
Grandfather got an oppertunity to say something disagreeable

to James about his watch, which his [James'] son, David, was carrying just now. [This] set James away in a huff. I tryed all I could to throw oil on the troubled waters, but I am affraid with little effect. I went away with him along to Phantassie [East Lothian] ploughmen's houses and ran back in time for the train. He got a grand night to go home – fine moon light.

Monday 17 December 1888

Poor Duncan has had a bad night. He got up at the same times, vomiting, and afterwards went into an unconcious state and remained so all morning. So, I set out for the doctor to East Linton [East Lothian] about half past eight, arriving at nine o' clock, [and] had to wait for him for a whole hour during which time I fretted very much indeed when I thought on the poor little boy lying screaming with pain while [the doctor] sat at his breakfast. But that was not all, for he [the doctor] had to attend a meeting at the poorhouse before coming out, and did not arrive till after eleven. But for that matter, I need not have cared. For he did not know what ailed poor Dow, but he gave a pre- scription for powders and went off saying he was in a very bad state. This, of course, we knew ourselves well. He kept scream- ing every quarter off an hour till midnight when he fell into a sleep and slept till morning.

Tuesday 18 December 1888

I think Duncan has got over his worst and appears to be better a good deal. So, we are wating anxiously the arrivle of the doc- tor, who arrived about eleven o'clock and asked very anxiously for his patient. So, I told him he was a good deal better I thought, as he had opened his eyes and given over screaming. So, he went into the house and after remaining twenty minutes, during which time he studdied the patient very attentively, he told me that the symptoms I took for better he took for worse, as they clearly showed he had had slight parallises of the brain and inflamation. And [he] told me to go to Biel [East Lothian] to Mr Muir – [the] gardener there – and get ice and put it on

[Dow's] head in a sow's bladder. [I was] not to let his head get
wet on any account. So, I was at my wits end for I could not get
away, there being no surfacemen on the length, only the ganger[49]
and he was at the east end. So, I sent Sandy with a letter to Mrs
Higgins to Ninewar [East Lothian] to see if she would allow
her gardener to go for it, which she did. [She] was very kind
and came down with it [in] her carriage to save time. During
the time the man was away I sent Sandy over to Kirklandhill
[East Lothian] to Mrs Forsythe for a bladder, which he got. So,
every thing being ready, we had the ice on by half past four. Mrs
Porter, hearing some one was ill, came along from Gateside.
She stationed herself by his bedside and attended him up till
half past nine when Bella and I stayed up till morning. We had
him removed before this to the room end and poor old grandfather had to shift to the kitchen. I was sorrow for him, for he
felt himself in the way. I suggested writing to Mary, my sister,
to come and take him away – as I knew she had a spare room.
But both Bella, my wife, and he are against me, so I have to give
in. This is the first time he has been put out of the best corner
of the house. But there was no other alternative as we must
keep Dow quiet, at what ever cost.

Wednesday 19 December 1888

I got Andrew Crooks to watch the gate till I ran up to Biel for
ice, and after coming down again we got a call from Inspector
Ross. So, I asked him if he would send a man to watch the gate
in the afternoon till I got a few hours sleep. So, he said, certainly, I could not work night and day. So, I got to bed for a few
hours a[nd] got up quite refreshed. The doctor had arrived in
the meantime and had given us no hope of [Dow's] recovery
unless his illness was the result of a stroke, which, of course, we
could not say. So, we were all naturally put about very much.
Mrs Porter was most attentive on him all day. And at night Mr
Porter came along to convay her home and stayed awhile and
gave us a very nice prayer for [Dow's] recovery, or for his soul
– if it was God's will to take him from us. So again, Bella and I

kept our lonely watch all night, with little hope in our hearts. During the night I wrote to Bella's sister, Helen, stating how we were placed and asking her mother to come as Bella was nearly done up with watching all night and working all day.

Thursday 20 December 1888

Duncan no better. At least, Doctor Gordon will not let us say it, or even hope. He says it is a most tretcherious disease but there was no hope of recovery unless it was an accident. If it was from natural causes, it was fatal. All this time I had the man in attendence on the gates, so that I went to Biel in the forenoon, and slept in the after. I had many anxious enquirers at the box and many offers of assistance from all quarters. Mr Higgins, Mrs Hamilton-Ogilvie's factor, told me that if there was anything in Biel House, or anything in his, I was to send or go and I would get them. Again, Mrs Porter watched over Duncan all day, and Mr Porter came and took her home and gave us another prayer, which soothed and cheered us up.

Friday 21 December 1888

I am very low spirited today and while I was up at Biel I could not keep the tears out of my eyes going up the road by myself. But on coming back I found Duncan was a little easier. But the doctor still saw none. Or, if he did, he would not admit it. At half past three o'clock p.m. Mrs McLachlan [Helen (Nell), sister-in-law] arrived from Portobello and she cheered us up a bit and declared [Dr] Gordon knew nothing about his trouble and was only trying experiments with [Dow]. But I would not give in to that. But she did a great deal of good to us at all events, and took a turn at watching at night and let Mrs Porter and Bella get a much needed rest, for they were both very hard up – Mrs Porter with a sore back, and Bella with fatigue and sleep.

Sunday 22 December 1888

We got a poor night of it with Andrew who was taken with the same symptoms as Duncan, and about the same time. So we fought with him and made him take phisic and poulticed his bowels till he fell asleep. I went along for the doctor to East Linton and told him I was afraid [Andrew] was taken with the same trouble as Dowie, and asked him to come out our way first thing. So, he promised to do so, but when he came he said [Andrew] had taken something which had disagreed with him and was little the worse. Was very glad to hear so, as I got a terrible fright. Duncan, poor fellow, seems better today, and Aunt Nell thinks he will soon be out of danger.

Sunday 23 December 1888

We got a surprise visit from David Kinnear [brother-in-law] from Inveresk [East Lothian] to take away grandfather. But he said he would rather go to the poorhouse as [David] had turned him out of his house before. So, as he said Jennie [sister] was going to be confined soon, I made that an excuse for refusing to let [grandfather] go. David went along the line to New Belton [East Lothian] to see old Daniel Stobo, an old master of his, to get a crack about farming. Duncan still keeps better and we are to be very sparing with the ice. Aunt Nell went off away home with the night train along with D K [David Kinnear]. Duncan cried a good deal, although she went out without saying good bye for fear of waking him. He was a little worse at night, with the crying, but let us hope he will be better in the morning.

Monday 24 December 1888

We all miss Nell today. She cheers up all she comes in contact with. I hope she got safe home and [is] nothing the worse of her two days jaunt. I went up to Biel for ice today as I did not wish to go on the morrow, being Christmas day [I] think there will be a good few gentry up at prayers at the chapel. I am glad to say Duncan is still keeping on improveing, although he is still greaving over his Aunt Nell's departure. We have recieved preasents from all hands and not a few Christmas cards. Also a letter from Portobello saying Nell got home all right, but found the old wife very frail. Grandfather is very frail but he [is] also very proud to say that he is to stay here. He does not wish to remove till he is carried to his grave, he said.

Tuesday 25 December 1888: Christmas Day

Nearly nineteen hundred years are gone since our blessed Saviour came to this earthly scene proclaiming peace and good will to man, who had forfeited his rights through Adam's. But God, who in spite of our stubborn and hardened hearts, so loved us that He sent His only son to die in our stead. So that He prepared a way for us to approach His divine presence through faith in Him and in Him alone. May He be ever near to strengthen and support through this weary world else we perish. By the way, Christmas is becoming more recognised as a holliday and day of rejoycing in Scotland than in former years.[50] Whitekirk Parish Church [East Lothian] was in this year again. Duncan still progressing.

Wednesday 26 December 1888

I recieved a great number of C[hristmas] cards yesterday, from friends far and near. It is a great comfort to us to think that we are not forgotten, although we are in such an isolated place. Duncan is still keeping what he has, poor little chap, but he is far from well. His pulse fluctuates very much and he is restless at night up till midnight. I always sit till two o'clock in the morning and waken Bella, who generally goes to bed at ten. Thus we divide the watch.

Thursday 27 December 1888

Things are going on pretty fair with Dowie. The doctor has stoped his bottles so I think that is a good sign, and no more ice.

Friday 28 December 1888

We are still keeping up our spirits. Duncan is improving – but not much. He gets a little milk food, but no other. Sometimes we may give him a little dry toast if he cries, but not unless. Grandfather is very hard up, poor old man.

Saturday 29 December 1888

I do not think Duncan is so well. His pulse looks high and he looks feverish. The doctor made some enquires about his bowels, and told Bella to move them either tonight or tomorrow morning. He gets worse about eight o'clock p.m. and asks for the ice bag on his head, which we keep on till past the turn of the night when he feels it cold and shakes it off himself. Gave him oil to move his bowels, as I think that is where the mischief is.

Sunday 30 December 1888

Duncan is very ill again and Dr Gordon orders his bottle to be renewed and given every six hours. Also, to keep the ice on his head – which we do. We got his bowels to move after a struggle. We gave him four times oil. Sandy went to East Linton for his bottle. Bella would not let me go for fear he might be wanting some thing just when someone came to the gate. Had a visit of W Tulloch from Tynninghame.

Monday 31 December 1888

Duncan seems better this morning, but was very ill all night. Old grandfather was very snappy, asking me if I was keeping him quiet and not allowing people to annoy [Dow] speaking to him. But after seeing [Dow], he came out quite pleased.

Tuesday 1 January 1889

Had a very quiet New Year's morning and old year's night, owing to Duncan's illness. We had no gysaits [guisers][51] which was a blessing. Was first footed by John Alexander, one of the surfacemen, at 8.30 p.m. Got a letter and cards for the boys from Alexander Ramage, also a packet of Launderine to wash with. Got the prize cock killed yesterday by the 3.30 [p.m.] NE express. We have recieved many marks of kindness from all our friends for which we have reason to thank God for his kindness and great mercies. May we prize such blessings as they deserve. Glad to say Duncan seems a great deal better today.
Andrew Ramage

Wednesday 2 January 1889

The great feast at Biel was the whole topic of conversation today. Everything went off beautifully, and everybody was well
behaved and enjoyed themselves splendidly. No one drunk, as
might have been supposed being New Year's day. I am glad to
say Duncan is still progressing favourably. Dr Gordon was well
pleased with him and he and grandfather had a long crack about
our genology, the French count and the Lady Isobell. The old
doctor thought him off his head a bit, I daresay. Took in my
potatoes in the afternoon – 1:1/2 bolls of good Champions,
which will save me 30 shillings at the preasent day prices. Had
a call off Mrs Higgins of Ninewar to see the boy. She brought
him a pitcher of nice sweet milk.

Thursday 3 January 1889

Our dear little boy has passed a quiet night and seems much
better to day. The doctor says he is going on fine and we are to
try him without medicine again. I hope he does not relapse this
time. Mr and Mrs Higgins called en passant and were asking
very kindly for him. Also Mrs Hope. […] Had a call off Robert
Faggo. Poor chap, his fingers are still very painfull. Grandfather
is very frail today. The sudden change from frost to fresh affects
him. He is always best in frost. Had a visit of Mary Jane McLean
on the old year's night. Poor lassy, she seems very frail. The
confinement is not good for her at her age, seventeen past six-
teenth of May. I went to [East] Linton with her at night.

Friday 11 January 1889

Grandfather is very ill today. He is gradually sinking weaker
and weaker, poor body. I sent away a poem to M J McLean.
My first production after the style of Rabby, Gordon says.
Duncan is going on fine now. He has been up a day or two and
soon we may expect to see him running about, if it be the will
of God.

Stenton Gates

My bonny lass I got yer letter
Yer cold I fear it is no better
Next time ye come when days are hetter [hotter]
And no sae short
[If] ye can only slip yer tether
We'll hae some sport

We'll trip it o'er to Auldhamstocks [Oldhamstocks]
And wi yer auntie and her folks
We'll wander down among the rocks
About the cove
Where when at school I learned to smoke
Like any stove

If we could wander at our wills
Upon the top o Hoprigg Hills
Or maby down by Dunglass Mills
Close to the sea
You there would soon forget your ills
And o'er the lea

Would skip it like an unbacked filly
Wi prancin step and right good [...]
Up Ettrickvale wi some young fellow
Y'ed stage it hame
Lord grant ye near may wear the willow
at Thirlstane [Thirlestane]

My best respects to yer auld mither
And all the same unto yer father
Yer Billie John wha is the scholar
And Kennie too
Likewise to Sammy wha's turned peeler
How do they do?

Tell them I hope to hear that Flora
Has now got o'er her midnight worry
Had aught come o'er her I bein right sorry
The bonny quines
So I hope that lang baith she and Rory
The brays may climbe

Wi gratefull heart I'm prood tae tell
Our Duncan's noo fast getting well
Ere lang we'll hae him at the school
Among the lane
Or sporting on the bank himsell
Wild as the wave

Grandfather's cough is very bad
And he's confined noo to his bed
Wi pillows propin up his head
To ease his breath
His hands and feet are cold as lead
Or liker death

So now my bonny Mary Jane
I'm glad to hear that you've got hame
Although you did mistake your train
And left yer brotch [brooch]
Had worse come o'er ye awa yer lane
'Twas nae reproach

And wishing you a glad New Year
And may you never shed a tear
But aye hae plenty o good cheer
Held to yer hankie
So I'll subscribe myself my dear
Your Uncle Andrew

Saturday 12 January 1889

Grandfather still keeps in a silent unconcious state, but seems easier today. Had a visit of A Johnston who used to be head carter at Biel. Poor chap, I was sorrow for him when he got the sack, but all will be no warning to him. He was very drunk tonight, but for a blessing he had his sister, Maggie, with him.

Monday 14 January 1889

I have never been from the door all day and have had a slight headache for want of a little exercise. Had a visit of W Tulloch from Tynninghame, and his brother from Edinburgh, and had a lively discussion on politics. Had a large meeting in the butt of ploughmen. All going to get a holiday tomorrow Hansel Monday.[52] George Forsythe is going to Edinburgh tomorrow so I got him to bring, or rather promise to bring, my father's bottle of cough mixture from McCallum of the Gras Market [Grassmarket]. Grandfather no better to day.

Sunday 20 January 1889

My father is no better to day. He has had a hard week of it with his cough and is still getting weaker. Poor old man. He suffers very much when it comes on him. Either Bella or I must be constantly in attendance on him. He gets so nervous when left himself. He would like if he could get any one to speak to him about his soul. I try my best, but he does not care for my logic, I can see. May God pardon his sins and recieve him into glory when his appointed time comes, be it soon or long. All the bairns are bad of the cold but they might be worse. Duncan is still keeping better so let us be thankfull to God for his mercies. I wrote two letters, one to my nephew, AR, and one to my sister, Jane. Also, Bella wrote to her mother – wonderfull as each succeeding year arrives.

Monday 28 January 1889

Grandfather seems stronger in body today, but his head seems

weaker. Have been digging nearly all day on the bank, very
tired. I saw by today's *Glasgow Herald* the General Boulanger
has had an overwhelming majority in Paris and now we may
expect rows with the ministry.[53] No news from Glasgow, Yours
Truely

Tuesday 29 January 1889
I have sent a letter to Jamie telling him [father is] no better,
poor body. He will never have it in his power to reproach me
for keeping him in ignorance of how his father was, or is. Although I doubt if he will thank me for my trouble. I have also
sent a few lines to William Edmond. Poor old William, he is
like myself on Parmasis [Parnasus] drunk.

> I heard a joke the other night
> About a man called Thomas Wright
> I'm told he had been at the Fair
> To see if he could get a hire.
> When up came Andrew the man
> Ha!, says he I hear yer been
> What ails ye at auld Mr C_K
> Weel and ye ken he's but a stink
> And kens nae mare about yer work
> Some time nae mortal man could please him
> At other times he is so pleasent
> Ye'd think he'd take ye in his bosom
> So ye ken I canny thole sic [...]
>
> Once more the natal day returns
> Of our imortal poet Burns
> And Scottish hearts in every land
> In mony a social friendly band
>
> Will meet together at their clubs
> Or in the parlour of the pubs

Or aiblins by some cronie's fire
They'll sweetly tune the Scottish lyre

Then sing his songs and sonnets [...]
Wi right good will and hearty glee
Beginning wi auld Tam O'Shanter
Wha hame fra Aire that night did canter   [Ayr]

They'll keep in mind to spare the dram
And gang as cloose hame as they can
The whiskey noo's no worth a sang
Few chiels can stand it very lang

It very seldom carries the beid
But jings it soon gangs tae your head
And make you act like ony bruit
Or gang and lye down in the street

And steals awa your greatest gift
So that of sense your fair bereft

　　　Mr Andrew Ramage

Wednesday 30 January 1889

I've been trying to dig, been at the saw
And I can settle at nane o the twa
For the nerves of my arm are tearin awa[54]
I can get nae rest wi them [at aa]

For my nerves are tearin just like the deil   [devil]
In fact I am a no very weel
And noo I mind upon the time
When I was young and in my prime

How I could wi the ablest work

And never yet was kent to shirk
Fair day or foul at six o'clock
I was at the face like ony cock

To navie both wi shool and barrow   [shovel]
To follow plough or brake or harrow
To drive a wood cart or a lorrie
Or yolk a janker or a carrie

I've handled pick and puice and hammer
And was respected by my ganger
To spike and gage he often set me   [physical work]
But to the van he ne'er wad let me   [would]

Till faith I got so cursed clever
I knocked his old hat to shiver
And then set aff into the toon
Where I fell in wi a nibor loon   [neighbour lad]

Wha at Portobello was a guard
Says he, [if] ye hae nae measured
For life or limb and care to try
To curse and swear and shout and cry
To run and shunt but mind your eye

Don't tell old W_m any lye
Tell him ye've …

Saturday 2 February 1889
Things look bad just now. Both my father and my wife are ill
and, as the old man is intirely dependent on her for every thing,
God grant she may not be laid up altogether. Let us be thankfull we are so well and rest in confidence that we may be able
to minister to the old man to the end. God will not put more
on us than we are able to bear. No word from Glasgow yet.

Wednesday 6 February 1889

We had Dr Gordon today and he says Bella has had a shock
of parallises of the face but will come all right again. But he is
coming back tomorrow in daylight to see her right. He was
nasty to me for not letting him know sooner, but the fault was
not mine as Bella thought it would come all right soon. Which I
trust it will, for she feels it very much, poor soul. I wrote away
to Glasgow to Alexander McLean to day. I hope he may answer
it soon. He is not up to much, but I think less of him than ever.
This is Dunbar Hirings Fair today. They have got a pretty good
day for a wander.

Thursday 7 February 1889

Recieved the parcel all right from Glasgow. Also a promise of a
£ on Tuesday next, from same source. Got a letter from sister
Mary asking for her father. Was sorrow I did not write, quite a
mistake. Was sure I had done till I got her letter. Father was bad
last night with pains in his back and sides, poor body. He will
not stand pain long. Wrote away today to Alick Ramage at
Springfield, Cockburnspath. Bella's head has been bad all day
but is much better now. Very cold all day. Hard frost, and all
the Glasgow trains were covered with snow so we will likely
get it before long. *AR*.

Friday 8 February 1889

This has been a sad day with me. Bella has not been able to lift
her head from the pillow all day with [a] sick headache. So, I
had to attend to my father – and the bairns. Make all the meat,
keep fires, tend hens, goat and rabbits – up till dinnertime, when
I got a man to look after the gate all afternoon. Dr Gordon's
bottle did her a deal of harm. Every time she took it she was
worse after. The doctor, an old scabby hielander, did not think
it worth his while to come back to see whether she was well or
ill, or if his medicine was doing her any good. But I hope I may
one day get the chance of paying him back in his own coin. This
is a fearfull night of snow and wind. We will soon have a block.

Saturday 9 February 1889

Weather very stormy. Snow drifting in exposed places. Temperature very low. No sign of change. If this frost continues the curlers will get to their waring play on Monday. But God help the poor labourers. They and their families will feel the pinch of hunger soon. My wife is much better today and able to be up again. My father is just the same. Meeting of bobbies [police] at 5.00 p.m. – Inspector Fraser absent. Sent PC Stenhouse from Bellhaven [East Lothian], Andrew Crooks at Edinburgh. Brought a pair of slippers for Angus but I am afraid they will have to be returned as they are too small.

Sunday 11 February 1889

Went to church at Prestonkirk to hear Mr M_ who has got into such hot water over his lecture on everlasting punishment. Got a very good sermon. Whatever his views are on our future punishment or reward, he can preach a very good sermon for our guidance and observance. In this preasent state I stayed at home all after noon and looked after the gate, as Bella was not very well and my father was really ill. But I was as well at home, the day being very cold. I had a call off [from] James Buchanan, George R_ and Thomas McDonald who often give me a call on the Sunday night for an hour or two.

> I hold it in my bounden duty
> To thank ye for yer welcome chicky
> You kindly sent yer Uncle Sandy
> Wha's failin fast

> To blythe kind hearted Mr Broon   [George Brown, cousin]
> Wha dwells into Kirkliston toon
> May every blessing be showered doon
> Upon your heady
> May your breek pouches ne'er be toon   [trouser pockets][torn]
> The friend in need

I'm sad to tell you that my father
Has nae prospects of gettin better
I think mysell that he wad rather
His end was here
But since he got yer winsome letter
He's taen some cheer
Wie gratefull heart improov to tell
Yer cheque we accept wi right good will.

Wednesday 20 February 1889

Great ball at Biel to the tennantry on all Mrs Ogilvie's estates. Special train from Edinburgh with all the hangers-on snugly ourio hawife. Nine omnibusses from Scott Croal & Sons to drive them from the station to the hall. Greenfield sent a man to assist me here, so I got two hours in my bed and was up in time for them returning from the spree.

Thursday 21 February 1889

Recieved a letter and cheque from my cousin George Brown, Kirkliston for ten shillings for grandfather. Very kind indeed.

Yours truly, A Ramage

Prematurely

I heard a joke the other night
How (ninepence) got an unco fright
And hirpled off wi a his might
And got the docter
To assertain gin a was right
Wi his bit dochter [daughter].

Auld Gordon grinned and shook his head
Say's he, guid man she'll soon be deed
So aff ye go wi a yer speed
And find a howdie
She'll get a job I think to cleed [clothe].

Some wee bit laddie
Prematurely says auld James
Since the world began it's been the same
It's a pitty that it had come hame
Prematurely

Monday 25 February 1889
Mary Jane McLean.

My poor old father has had a bad day today
Andrew Ramage

Thursday 28 February 1889
Very cold day

On February the twenty eight
I sit and shiver out of sight

And in my cabin I stick fast
To bield me fra the bitter blast

My mind dwells mostly on the time
When I did whirl along the line

Whiles up and doon the hill to father
And sometimes on as far as Gala

The toon whare once they selt the Kirk
Which stands upon the banks o Ettrick.

Where often I hae dreamed my dreams
As I sat gazing in its streams

Andrew Ramage

Thursday 28 February 1889

The situation remains unaltered. The weather is very stormy.
The wind keeps still in the east, so we may look for a few gales.
No news from any of our friends.

1 March 1889

> The snoe east wind blows quite a gale
> The snow lies thick o'er hill and dale
> The birdies chirp their woefu tale
> So piteously
> While goatie nibbles at her bale
> Contentedly
>
> At school my twa bit laddies run
> And snow ba[ll] other[s] in their fun
> They are as happy gin the sun
> Was shines bright
> Their race of life is but begun
> And ever light

2 March 1889

The snow storm continues and further east and south seems to
be pretty severe. Had a letter from R_ and found all well at
home, but bad news from Allness.

To Mrs McLachlan

> Dear Nell
> I own I am your debtor
> For twice you've sent me a bit letter
> In which you state our Duncan's better
> I'm prood to hear't
> He'll likely want to stay fur lang
> I'm rather feart

Wi gratefull heart I'm proud to tell
The rest of us are keeping well
Sandy and George both at the school
Amoung the lane
Or sportin on the bank themsell
Wild as the wave
My father he's still very bad
Indeed it's sometimes very sad
To look upon him in his bed
He lies so still
We often think his heart has ceased
To beat at all

Give my kind love to our auld mother
Also the same unto our father
Your brother, Sand, I'm glad he's better
And Nellie too

My dear kind-hearted sister, Nell
I'm proud to hear that Duncan's well
I ken ye'll keep him like a swell
Both you and Granny.

I hope she's keeping like hersell
Both her and Sanny
Wi gratefull heart I read your letter
In which you state you all are better

The Nor-east winds they blaw sa bitter
But by and by
When sol has mounted up an far hother
Shines in the sky
His cheering influence you'll feel

And mad like bairnies frae the school
Ye'll sport and run like ony fool

Along the sands
As happy as gin ye were gatherin wool
On solid land

His cheerin influence you'll find will soon
Bring health and gladness to your toon
As warm and brightly he smiles doon
Upon the sand
May some kind fairie waft a goon.

Wi magic wand
To sport and find
To you who've proved yourself so kind
And never failed to keep in mind

That fortune often doesna send
A[ll] we wad like
But gin she send once parted friends
We need na like

Gie my respects to our old father
Also the same unto our mother
And when ye gang to see yer brother
At ony time
Tell him but deed I need na bother

It's but wasts o time
For weel I ken the chield man wall
And may bitter pills man swallow
The darenae weell make freinds fair follow

When H_ish Nell
Or some kind broonie fra the hills
Send ane frae Innerleithen Mills
Where Tweed in gentle eddying rills
Runs to the sea

They have no debtors duns or bills
To bother wie

Had I the power I'd send wi speed
To you who are the friend indeed
That came to help us in our need
An o the best
I'll ne'er forget whin Dunci's head
Was at it's worst

Poor Belle and I were both forlorn
Untill upon you smileing morn
Your preasance did our [home] adorn
And cheer us both
Thou art the heart o real good corn
I'll gie my oath

So may blind fickle fortune still
Keep you and yours in plenty till
Yer yiblins [able to] start a paper mill
In Portobello
Then who can doubt but Robert's skill
Will be heard till

And now dear Nell you'll like to hear
The both of us are in good cheer
The bairns are well our only fear
So for my father.

Lord grant his end may draw us near
To one another
Give our kind love to your old father
Also the same unto your mother
And when you write unto your brother
In New South Wales
Tell him that his Belle will send a letter

If nothin fails
So now good luck attend you all
And should misfortune ere befall
Show me the way to turn the ball
Ye may depend
Quickly take her to the hall
Or other end

Andrew Ramage

Recieved from Police Inspector Fraser
A square of good tobacco leaf
If there's an ounce I'm sure to a quarter
And I'm as proud as gin it been beef

'Twill keep me smokin for a week
And save me of a bob at least
So I will just enjoy my reek
As well as gin it had been a feast
For weel I ken he doesna meet

For he has plenty aye to spend
His wife or weans to be so kind
And then he disna toil or sweat
Nor has he ought to cause his mind
To ere regret such gifts to me

So I will thankfully accept his gift
So thankfully I will accept
His gift and may he happy be
And may the powers above protect
Him safe and sound this very night
When he's patrolin through the toon
And ayblins tackled in a fight
Wi some course drunken fisher loon

Andrew Ramage

Wednesday 13 March 1889
On this 13th day of March

> Now when the crow begins to search
> I sit me doon to wile the time
> And write a verse or twa in rhyme
> Dim backward as I cast my eye
> What varied scenes before me lie
>
> The most of them sad to tell
> Are no great credit to mysell
> For I was thoughtless young and gay
> And had na parents to obey
>
> But ran my course wild as the wasie
> Wastin my substance among the lave
> Wha wanton cast their time away
> On pleasures which but last a day
>
> So now I lonley sit and nourse   [nurse]
> For things hae taen anoner turn
> Still I am blessed compared wi some
> I have a wife and five wee sons.
>
> A daughter too a bonny hen
> A cossey house both but and ben
> So I will thank the Lord in heaven
> For what He here on earth has given

This day our youngest boy is one year old, and a stout little
fellow he is at his age. What a change in the weather since this
day twelve month. Then we had snow all round us. Now the
mild west wind threatens to give us a shower of March dust[55]
so much valued by the farmers that a handfull is compared to
handsfull of gold. My father, poor body, has had a bad night

77

and looks very ill this morning. He says he is [waving adieu] to the Land of the Leel[56] and he does not know where it is. May God in his mercy recieve his soul in heaven through the re-deeming blood of Jesus Christ, who suffered and died for just such sinners as he. I am glad to say, when he is conscious, he can camly await his end in that hope.

> The ancient ruined castle of Dunbar
> Against whose rugged sides the billous wars
> Has long withstood the grinding shock
> Sometimes waves, sometimes of rock
>
> As the mighty billows in their sport
> Breaks rudely gainst her with angry snort
> Dunbar's old ruined castle stands
> Has stood for ages long
> And many a noble gallant band
> Have bled to keep her strong
>
> But now the Provost of the town
> And baillies ane and all
> Are clamouring to tear her down
> For fear that she may fall
>
> I were bitter they should all combine
> And prop up the noble pile
> And not like dirty grovelling swine
> By every trick and wile
>
> Endeviour to persuade the fools
> Whose votes support them at the poll
> That she'll no tumble in the pools
> That round her whirle and roll
>
> Endeviour to perswade poor voters
> She's a danger to their weans

That one day she'll tumble in the breakers
Or burst their ain big wames

There was men their nae mind
Wha slight the grand old walls
Where our fathers and their countrymen
Withstood the English balls
As they fought for liberty and life
With Black Duglass in command
And when again his gallant wife
Refused to let them land

As they gaze upon the crumbling pile
Do they no transports feel
Or dream they see the soldiers file

And rank at duties cale   [kale]
To brandish round the deep died steel
In long and sturdy blows
While back recoiling seems to reel
Their beaten southern foes

But no, the cowardly craven crew
Their only wish is to be with them
And that they could join the chosen few
That compose our Parliament

*   *   *

At Biel there was a tennant's ball
To take […] they […] call
The farmers flocked both big and small
To mix wi gentry
And well they filled the ancient hall
And cleaned the pantry

A special train frae Embro toon
Brought many an old sneck-drawin loon
Wha's wife was decked in braw new goon
To get a fill
I wat they looked bath lank and toom
As up the hill
In Croal's old omnibusses they sat
For once did ride and didna pay
That was the reason they smiled so gay
The wisent hags
They kenned they'd nought to do or say
But fill their bags.
Mrs Ogilvey she sat and smiled so sweet
Said she was proud that day to meet
And tennants and neighbours frankly greet
For their great kindness

Monday 18 March 1889

My father died today at 9.00 a.m. Poor old body. His was a
happy release from pain and suffering. May his soul be recieved
in glory through the intersession of Jesus our Lord and Saviour
in whose inodiation he placed his belief and hope for eternity. I
made arrangement to inter him in Prestonkirk Churchyard East
Linton [East Lothian].

Tuesday 19 March 1889

Went to Portobello and saw the old folks and then to Edinburgh
and saw Mr and Mrs Watters and called at Hunter & Co, but
did not see Mr McIntosh.

Wednesday 20 March 1889

This day I have interred the mortal remains of my dear father in
Prestonkirk. All my friends being present – that is my immeadi-
ate friends and near relations. And such a fearfull day of wind
and rain. We were all wet to the skin, some of us twice. They

were, some of them, very kind in helping to defray the expences, others never mentioned [this]. I had what would do my turn, let me be thankfull. Many a thought, many an anxious thought [this] gave the poor old man that is gone – along with my self – but God is a bountyfull provider. They that trust in Him shall never want. *AR*.

Thursday 21 March 1889

I went to Dunbar [East Lothian] today to the Registrar to register my father's death and got a certificate to the gravedigger which it appears should have been presented to him before burrial under a penalty of 1£, but which he told me he did not require.[57] So the fault was not mine, as it was done in ignorance. Old Comb is very particular about these things, but I hope I may not often need to go his way on the same errand. I saw a wreck at Bellhaven Rocks but there was no lives lost, so that will be a great credit to the Dunbar life boat men. Mr Deans of H W Sicks has a dead horse lying on the road side.

Thursday 21 March 1889

> O sweet be thy sleep in the land of the grave
> In Preston Kirkyard on the banks of the Tyne
> While we thy loved offspring in sorrow will rave
> Of thy love and thy kindness in the days of lang syne
> Thy partners asleep far off in Cockpen
> Along with the sons of her Saviour
> And thy wish oft expressed was whatever did pass
> You'd be laid there at rest some fine morrow
> Still thou knew at the last of thy sojurn
> That to that loved spot thou would never return

Sunday 24 March 1889

Went to church today and saw my father's last resting place. It is hardly recognizeable now. The gravedyger has made a very good job of it, so I will employ him to sort it up a bit and put in a few spring flowers. I got a letter from Mary today, making an apology for her last letter. Poor soul, she need not have troubled.

> My poor old father we did lay
> In Preston Kirk cauld in the clay
> Where all must rest till Judgement Day
> When we shall rise say
> When the dread trump shall sound and
> Up to the skies
> Before the throne of God to stand
> A motely throng from sea and land
> And hear your doom by his command
> For all your sins
> O may we take our Saviour's hand
> And then will rise.

> *   *   *

> O sweet be the sleep in the land of the G_
> My dear aged father for ever
> For ever, ah no, let not man be a slave
> His hopes from existance to sever

> Though cold be the clay where thon
> Pillow thy head
> In the dark silent mansions of [our] Saviour
> The spring shall return to thy low narrow bed
> Like the beams of the day star tomorrow

> Thy partner's asleep in lovely Cockpen
> Near the home of thy childhood and youth

While thy flower of us all, thy much loved son, Stephen
Who defended his country his friend and the truth
Was laid in Co'path in the prime of his life

Thy Mary's asleep near the house of the Lord
The home of thy childhood and youth
While two were cut off in the pride of their life
                                                    [Stephen and George]
And a third one was taken in youth   [Alexander]

We thy fond children must sighings give
The dark silent mansions of sorrow
And look back on the days that will never return
And wish for this life's latest morrow

Thy Mary's asleep near the place of thy b_
While thy children are scattered far and near
They like thee are returned to their own hearth
When their sojurn was over down here

Let us hope that you all are united above
In the mansions of glory and light
If so we're content to picture thy Mary
As you gaze on that face resplendent the sign

Of our Saviour who left his heavenly abode
And so lowly was born in a stable
That he might reconcile us once more to our God
For 'twas more than frail mankind was able
And we the loved children.

Had a visit off W Tulloch today. His wife, Jean, has been very
ill but she is now recovering. Poor soul, she has had a long spell
of it. Poor Wattie is very proud to think she is getting on so
well. He has had his niece staying staying with him – keeping
his house for him – which was a good thing for him under the

circumstances. He threw his bread on the water and it has returned after many days. He brought her up when she had no home and now she is nobly endeviouring to repay him and his canty wifie, Jean. It's an old saying and a true one – 'kindness begets kindness'. Yours Truly,

Andrew Ramage
Stenton Railway Gates

Monday 25 March 1889

Stenton Railway

Today we got two painters from Baileyfield to clean the house – which has been to be done for four years. Just like them, two men came by the first train and carried along the half of their tools and then took their breakfast for an hour. After doing so, they went back to East Linton for the rest of their tools and at eleven or so they have not returned. So, by the time they arrive it will be time for dinner, then a snack and then away for the train. So, that two men took a whole day to carry their gibbles from East Linton. No wonder the Company is poor.

Stenton Crossing

Tuesday 26 March 1889

We have had two painters today again from 9.00 a.m. First performance – one hour for breakfast. Next, washed and painted the roof and a small portion woodwork of doors and window. Then one other hour for dinner, then finished the doors and window and gave the new wood of the eves one coat. Then quit at 5.00 pm.

Stenton Crossing

Tuesday 26 March 1889

> Is there a [one …] fool
> Owre fast for thought, owre hot for rule
> Owre blate to seek, oure prood to serve
> Let him draw near

And owre this grassy heap [sit doon]
And drap a tear
'Twas on the twentieth day of March
In grace and Eight Nine
Yours Truly
Rabbie Burns

As I sit poorin owr this book
Searchin my brains for words to write
A look at Burns and then I shook
My stupid head
Thinks I, I'd better take a dook
In the damn Lead   [Lead burn]

For I'll ne'er learn at ony time
To write in either prose or rhyme
I'd better try some other [...]
Far o'er the sea
At this I'll never make a drive
It's no for me

Wednesday 27 March 1889

Today I have wrote a letter to the General Post Office in Montreal, Canada, making enquiries about my brother, William, so that I may intimate to him the death of our father.[58] But I'm afraid it's a wild goose chase. He has hisself to blame. For I wrote to him last and got no reply. Perhaps he is not alive, poor chap. He was never strong after going out there.

   Yours Truly, Andrew Ramage

Saturday 28 March 1889

I had a long arguement with John M Williams about Home Rule. John is a Scotch-Irishman and a Nationalist and is greatly against the present Tory government, and especially the Liberal Munnisto. I was very large on the times and Piggott. He did not

85

like what I said about Sir William Harcourt in his attack on Sir R Webster, but just boo-ed me out of the face of it, as the Parnell-lites are so fond of doing in the House of Commons daily.[59]

Mr Parnell said a few bitter things of Lord Salisbury today but of course he was not there to reply and [Parnell] had the whole thing his own way. He is a very cool and clear speaker is Mr Parnell, and does not often speak without a purpose. So Jock and I had to leave off politics and start a subject we could speak on without getting in a rage. I very nearly let James Hamilton through in front of the BK goods [train] and that would have put an end to his old cabbie. I had a visit off old Joe Baillie, and he and Jock M Williams fell out and so he went off in high dudgeon. Jock told him he was like every other English man, all belly and talk.

Tuesday 2 April 1889

Seventh day of the painters. Poor souls, they have a long day of it from six o'clock till five at night. Their work is not very heavy, but it is very tiresome and requires a great amount of patience and skill. Still, seven days seems a fearfull amount of time to clean and paint two rooms and a bed closet. But, if the railway company do not grudge or find fault, I need not trouble about it. They are two very nice and obliging chaps and are making a first class job of it. They are going to take all week, which at twenty five shillings per week makes 2£ 10s without counting paper and paint.

> O saw ye ought o Mrs Clark
> Stumpin about without a sark
> And wi auld Jamie [in] the dark
> About the Mains
> They're jumpin other for a lark
> Just like twa wanes
>
> Man yon was just a woesome sight
> To see the carlin in skin tight

Dancin about and showin fight
At ilka turn
I saw mysell here take a flight
Out o'er the burn

Twa w[ee] auld farrant dumie chiels
Wha dub them selves as painters

Andrew Ramage
His book
April 2 1889

DIARY

Part II
(1914–1917)

Lachie and Andrew,
Edinburgh, November, 1916.

Sunday 26 July 1914

Inspector Lewis with flying squad putting in new sleepers. Made an awfull hash of my flower beds. They were in an awfull hurry at first, but stuck for want of chains.

Monday 27 July 1914

Murray, Blaikie and Dickson at 10.00 a.m. Murray had two of Curr's men in the lock up on Saturday night. Ballast train stopped in section twenty minutes without being pinned on to train on line. Very slack way of working block.[60]

Tuesday 28 July 1914

Bob Dickson at 10.30 a.m. Bob at North Berwick for his kist and tools. Big squad still here lifting cattle. Special Engine No. 888 went over caution at forty miles per hour. Tam D and J Craig half hour feeding on my berrie[s] en passant when they should have been working. Peter White cutting hay in west bank. Jeffry away home at 2.00 p.m. for mail train.

Wednesday 29 July 1914

Murray and Dickson [policemen] at 8.30 p.m. Jamie here from Haddington [East Lothian] – left at 9.00 p.m. Letter from Angus. He got home all right at 10.00 o'clock. Called on Aunt Nell and found all well. Flying Squad here and cleaned up the berry bushes. Old Willie Johnson down in his ain trap. Mr White finished his hay cutting. W W Hope and Mrs Hope motored up the brae with an old wife sitting behind. Bob got his trunk up from North Berwick – in post cart from station.

Thursday 30 July 1914

Inspector Lewis here with his men at 10.00 a.m. Left for the mail from Edinburgh at 2.00 p.m. Tennant here to see about a train being twenty minutes between Belton Ford and Linton on the nineteenth inst. Bob started with Mr Frazer. George Chirnside at 7.30 a.m. Bob Dickson passing to Tynninghame. Bowling – Bick got knocked out. So much for Coltart. Bella at the sea but [...] was back. Cycle smash head of Tynninghame road. Anderson Hedlywick ran into George Aitken, Traprain.

Friday 31 July 1914

Great excitment with the surfacemen stopping trains with the bogie. Very nearly stoped the 3 o'clock fast [train] taking up sleepers to Linton. Neddy roused Miss Balfour. Away home to Whittinghame in Denholm's car. P White puting up his hay in West Bank. Flags taken off after three weeks cautioning. Am very glad to see them done. Lot of sailor men off to join their ships at Isle of Wight, ready for war. German looking child takin notes a[ll] day. Away hame by the 4.[o]7.

Saturday 1 August 1914

Denholm and his men cleared all the sleepers away from the gate to the opposite side of the line. Young Tom on the road. Meet[ing] of police at 4.30 p.m. Full meet – except Murray. Woman with glass eye wanted name of Swan. Old Welsh here – had to go away without money. Drills to be measured on Monday. Bob away to Haddington. Lachie put out lamps. J Edmont's men working here all forenoon. Knowes [Farm] workers cleaning hedge on the road side.

Sunday 2 August 1914

Uncle Roderick [here] from Selkirk. Took a walk up to Biel with him and Ella [Sandy's daughter], and lay about all day after.

Monday 3 August 1914

News of war. Germany against Europe – our folks to be involved. We are to fight for Belgium neutrality.

Tuesday 4 August 1914

Reservists and Teritorials called out so Angus and Willie must go. Poor chaps, but some one must go.

Wednesday 5 August 1914

Angus passed at 1.00 p.m. for London, to join his regiment [Scots Guards, 2nd Battalion] – so he's off to the Front. Willie away to Dunbar with the [Lothian and Borders Horse] Yeomanry. Rorie came home by the 2.2 ex[press] Edinburgh. Two hundred Teritorials here from Linlithgow at Phantassie, all cyclists. Company of them at West Barns and motor dispatch riders flying all round. Flying squad men not to get their pay. No money, banks all shut. Some grumbling.[61]

Thursday 6 August 1914

Lot of lying rhumours in the papers about battles. The Belgium army has checked the Germans from crossing their country into France. We hurry up our mobilization, ready to go to their help. Austria has declared war on Russia. Italy remains neutral. Naval activity at Orkney. Great victory for Britain, but unconfirmed.

Friday 7 August 1914

Bob saw Willie at Dunbar. He is waiting on a horse. They go to Haddington. Great battle at Orkney denied by Mr Churchill in House of Commons. Great row with T Denholm and Neddie. Four of Jeffrey's men came back late and drunk. They are all away home with their boggies [bogies].

Saturday 8 August 1914

Tam Hume on the road. All the men here … rain. Sogers

looking for German spies, searchin motor cars. Linton Boys at Markle Main all day. Rorie went away.

Sunday 9 August 1914

Major C K Brown and his son and daughter walked out here and found [the] misses out, as usual. Lachie at Haddington and saw Jamie, but not Bill. Motor cyclist got a spill running into yeomanry horses. Turning very few machines up here. Mrs Conally doon.

Sunday 9 August 1914

Bob and Lachie at Haddington. Willie up there – been at Duns for horses. Searching cars at Linton and Tynninghame for German spies. Motor cyclists came to grief with yeomanry horses turning in front of them. Was up watching [the] ships scouting about in mouth of the Firth of Forth. Very few troop trains. C K Brown here with his son and daughter. Bella and Ella out when they came – as usual.

Monday 10 August 1914

Rainie got away Bill's cape for James Walker. Lot of war news. Great fighting in Alsack Loraim [Alsace Lorraine] in France. Thirty thousand German and fifteen thousand French slaughtered. Been busy all day. Sogers still searching motors. Letter from Sandy and Aunt Nell. All well with both. Lachie got his byke from J Smith, new. Old chain wheel and pedal. Charman up the brae on motorbike. W W Hope and his misses motoring about. Also Tam I Dods doon with cycle for fear of looseing his pony.

Tuesday 11 August 1914

T Denholm away up to see Lewis. They are, they say, going to watch the Lady's Bridge. Angus sent home his clo's [clothes] and boots by train. Uncle Roderick came by the last train from Duns. They are all well. Lots of cycles and motors flying about watching spies. One caught at Haddington – Cullen, the road surveyor's son-in-law, who was riding about in the country.

Wednesday 12 August 1914

Grouse shooting begins. The gentry have something to think about this year. Wrote a letter to Angus. Perhaps he may not get it, but I've done my best.

Thursday 13 August 1914

Ballast train lifting sleepers left sixteen lying here. Jamie D_ kicking up a row. Jamie doon frae Haddington. He is well. They are sto[p]ping everyone coming through. Lord Binning[62] is asking them their questions.

Friday 14 August 1914

Wrote to Aunt Nell and Sandy. Soger patching byke. Got two bags coal from H Lunem by Scott Biel carter. Germans are getting the worst of the fighting in Belgum and France. Trains of soldiers passing to the war. Found a flag of the 2nd Sherwood Forresters [2nd Battalion Sherwood Foresters]. Mr White at Bellhaven for his sister and neice. T Denholm at West Barns with Vietch when John Edmond was down seeking him to sign a circular.

Saturday 15 August 1914

Ran up to Linton and reported instruments not working. They were all right when I came back. T Denholm keept guard when I was away. Full meet of police 4.30 p.m. Instruments working intermittently. Bob got the sack, no work. Tom Curr going on the post for Peter. He was round with him today learning the road. Not much news from the Front. Germans still being turned back in Belgium.

Sunday 16 August 1914

Trains run all day with soldiers from the north – Aberdeen,

Inverness, Fort George and Perth. Stayed at home all day, old
Bob Haddin keept me company. Hogg (linesman) [here] sorting
instruments. Signed his sheet for Saturday under protest – been
sorry for it ever since. Lachie lay about all day.

Monday 17 August 1914

Letter from George [son]. He wants Lachie to go to Moosomin
[Saskatchewan, Canada] to his [George's] brother-in-law to finish
his time as a blacksmith and motor mechanic. But allas, it's so
far – too dear a passage. British troops landed in France. Big
battle yesterday.

Tuesday 18 August 1914

Letter from Andrew – he is well. Bella wrote Jean and Eliza.
Master Alick Kinloch in scout dress. Lot of sogers flying about,
exchanging places.

Wednesday 19 August 1914

Willie down from Haddington. He is well and volunteered for
active service.

Thursday 20 August 1914

Making preperations for Ella going home [to Capesthorn,
Cheshire].

Friday 21 August 1914

Bella away to Capesthorn by 8.54. I am boss till she comes back.

Saturday 22 August 1914

Aunt Nell and Adam [her son] arrive from Portobello. Adam
very drunk but we keept him from going [to] Linton again.

Sunday 23 August 1914

Great battle going on in Belgium. Lord Leven and Melville

wounded and The Scots Greys cut up. Adam, very quiet, went away alright. Willie down last night for clean clos [clothes].

Monday 24 August 1914

Bella from Capesthorn all right, and left all well.

Tuesday 25 August 1914

Bob Dickson at 10.30 a.m and 5.00 p.m. Two thousand British lost at the Battle of Mons in France. Arnott at Lewis.

Wednesday 26 August 1914

Tennant sent for The Pink mobilisation circulars which I sent in with Johnie Watson. Murray [and] Dickson at Whitekirk.

Thursday 27 August 1914

Chirnside at Whitekirk at 7.20 a.m. Letter from Aunt Nell. Eliza J D at Linton all afternoon.

Friday 28 August 1914

John Edmond measuring the Lady's Brig again. Jamie took away up oil cans. Old Curr's showing a spy the road up the hill. Donald the Keeper away doon on his byke. Johnie Watson and Archie Sandors keept waiting for quarter of an hour. Gave old Mrs White away her bottle of whisky. She said it was nae for her and a mistake – what an old liar she is. Kirklandhill [Farm] and Knowes [Farm] both leading in wheat.

Saturday 29 August 1914

Full meeting of police at 4.30 p.m. T Denholm on the road himself. Lot of folks making noise coming home frae Linton. Very wet afternoon. Lot more of our sogers being mown down. Naval victory at Heligoland.[63]

Sunday 30 August 1914

Very wet day, although Jamie down from Haddington. He got a

wet night to go home in. No word of Willie going away yet.
Every one speerin about Russians passin here the night [...].

Monday 31 August 1914

Six thousand British killed and wounded in four days fighting
in France. P C Murray and Whitekirk – new man. Letter from
Aunt Nell. She has been at Heiton [Roxburghshire] seeing auld
[spinsters] Miss Innes and Miss Tunnard. Asking about Russians
passing here etc. Tynninghame van horse ran away up at Biel –
broke man's face and hurt his back and arm. W Borthwick and
T Reid went up and brought down man and horse, and estate
carter went up later and brought down the van. Some foreign
looking P_s up the brae on cycles.

Tuesday 1 September 1914

Great battles going on with our troops in France – awfull
carnage. Letter from Sandy – all well.

Wednesday 2 September 1914

Germans not into Paris yet but trying hard and very hard hit.
Docharty away to [en]list I hear. Never been at his work. Last
night, wrote to Sandy telling him not to list but stay at home
and mind his wife and family.

Thursday 3 September 1914

Docharty not out yet. Chirnside on his job for going away with
James Smith's byke.

Friday 4 September 1914

Dickson and Cockburn at 10.30. Docharty's father lifting firewood sleepers. Old Rose watching the Lady's Bridge. Got a war
map from Jean and had to pay 2d for it. Wrote to Aunt Nell.
Farmers leading in corn. J Curr going to Garvald next week.

Saturday 5 September 1914

Dickson and Cockburn at 4.30. Willie down for clean clothes. He looks well and is healthy.

Sunday 6 September 1914

Took a turn down to Bellhaven for sand. Did not stay long. Bob at the Kirk. Soldiers will be busy fightin the day. Mrs Johnston doon at the Kirk. Old B drove her up in his trap.

Monday 7 September 1914

Mrs H Ogilvy is offering ten shillings per week to her men to fight for her but na, they're no there for that, but lookin for a better job.

Tuesday 8 September 1914

Meet of police at 5.30. Murray, Dickson and Cockburn.

Tuesday 8 September 1914

Had a dram from Bill Middlemass, who was up dipping lambs. Also had a dram wi G Cockburn and T Denholm.

Wednesday 9 September 1914

Got a nip from George Cockburn. Chirnside at 9.15 a.m. [taking] signature. Some spies in woman's clothes. Wrote to Aunt Eliza [sister-in-law]. Got a few lines from Aunt Nell. Bob at Sunnyside Jaffray. Sent away a lot of rams to the sale at Edinburgh.

Thursday 10 September 1914

Bella and I diggin taties but they are very small.

Friday 11 September 1914

Bella at Edinburgh – Portobello. Got boots from Jackson for Willie and Bob. Chirnside and Cockburn. Chirnside going to Dunbar.

97

Saturday 12 September 1914

31 years since I lost my right arm at Portobello. Chirnside and Cockburn at 10.20. Letter from Angus. He is still at the Tower of London. Jean is well. Have an awfull sore back.

Sunday 13 September 1914

Went to church and found old Tarnie greetin as usual. Had Bob Dickson and Cockburn at 3.30 p.m. Touser up the brae wi her wee sisters. Wrote to Angus and Aunt Nell. Met Mr Williams Hope at Phantassie hinds' houses. He looks as skinny as usual. Mrs McDonald at the Kirk too.

Monday 14 September 1914

Wrote to Angus. No word from Sandy or any of the others. Meeting of police at 4.30 p.m. (full). Willie here from Haddington. He is looking well and getting on fine.

Tuesday 15 September 1914

Tam Hume away up the brae on his byke. [He] thinks he's to be taken off the bridge watching.

Wednesday 16 September 1914

Jamie from Haddington. He is uncomfortable with his landlady since he had the row about his grub.

Thursday 17 September 1914

George Chirnside at 2.00 p.m. Taking signature. P C Cockburn at 10.00 p.m. Meet Murray, Bellhaven. T Denholm here – dinner.

Friday 18 September 1914

Letter from Sandy. His boy, Alick, is ill. He says sore throat and [is] ran down in body. Papers from Jean (army and navy).

Saturday 19 September 1914

Chirnside, Dickson and Cockburn at 5.00 p.m. T Denholm here packing up. Joint letter from Rosie – all well.

Sunday 20 September 1914

Bella and Lachie at the Kirk to hear George [...] preach. Old Jamie at Stenton. Lay about all day.

Monday 21 September 1914

Bob Dickson at 8.00 p.m. No one else turned up a [...] at Tynninghame road end. Adam Johnston started with T Denholm. Mr Johnston doon frae Biel sellin something. Wrote to Sandy at Buxton [Derbyshire].

Tuesday 22 September 1914

Cockburn at 8.30 p.m. Mrs Stenhouse taking away a cockerel. Lachie beating with Sir Archibald Buchan Hepburn of Smeaton at Hailes. T Hume out cutting hedges. Three gunboats sunk in North Sea by German submarine. Also six merchants sunk in bay of Bengal by German light cruiser, Emden.

Wednesday 23 September 1914

Letter from Jean. She is well. George Chirnside at 2.30. Got in all my sleepers. T Denholm packing up joints in front of cabin. No great news from the continent army. Not making much progress.

Thursday 24 September 1914 –

Friday 25 September 1914 –

Saturday 26 September 1914

Lachie listed into the Royal Scots Territorials.[64]

Sunday 27 September 1914

Very quiet here. Lachie looks sad.

Monday 28 September 1914

Letter from Sandy. Jean and Angus all well. Angus diggin trenches at Lyndhurst Camp. Waiting on [the] Gordons. Write a reply at once for fear he may flit soon to seat of war.

Tuesday 29 September 1914

Pay day. Sent away my orders for stores. Mrs Ogilvy coming to Biel tomorrow. Old Curtis home to get things ready.

Wednesday 31 September 1914

Wrote Sandy and Jean. Peter White thrashin of his corn in [the] field. Sam Brown and James Currie with squad helping. Very cold day. T Denholm cutting hedges. Old Rose not up to much, poor old man.

Thursday 1 October 1914

Cockburn at 10.30 a.m. Bella at Howmuir. Lachie – postcard asking for his greatcoat. Also letter from Aunt Nell.

Friday 2 October 1914

Babtie, Kirkland Hill brought a lot of [rye] bags for Howmuir [Farm]. James Jamson and Bobbie […] came doon for them later and brought doon four bags [o stuff]. The wife went up and filled in the afternoon.

Saturday 3 October 1914

Geordie Chirnside at 2.30 p.m. en route to Tynifield. Lachie doon fra Haddington an filled his boots wi tackits. He's gey quail lookin but likes the sogerin fine, he says. Tamie Denholm and his wife and cousin pooin brambles in Ninewar Wood. Wylie's motor up at six o'clock (a.m.) wi a millman, and came back for him at night. Very quiet day wi me at the gates. Bob put out my lamps. A Johnston on the road. Nae sogers the day here. Letter frae Jean. She's havin a quiet day or twa.

Sunday 4 October 1914

Lay about all day. No word from anyone. Bob went and brought the newspapers, but there is no news. Stephen Ramage [nephew] passed to Hamstock Mains.

Monday 5 October 1914

Letter from Angus with £1.10 enclosed. He is off for the war, he says, by the signs of the times. Bob Dickson and Cockburn at 10:30 a.m. Bob ill all night with his teeth and head. Tom Curr on the Stenton post for this week – he goes away to a place next.

Tuesday 6 October 1914

Went up and saw old Ho-Ho about coal. So I got a good big load at 4.40 which took Bella and I an hour to put in. Cleaned out my midden and emptied a bed of chaff. A last letter from Angus from on board ship at Southampton, bound for the continental war. But he doesn't know where, poor chap. We may never hear from him again so we can only wish him 'God speed' and commend him to His care.

Wednesday 7 October 1914

Got half a crown from Dr Marjoribanks, Stenton. Also a bob from a lady en passant. Cockburn Whitekirk at 8.00 p.m.

Thursday 8 October 1914

Bob Dickson awa to East Linton cattle market, Simpson Hedderwick,[65] left his byke here at shed. [...] Rintoul left Irvine for his thrashing mill when it came doon frae Meiklings.

Friday 9 October 1914

C C Col Borthwick buried today. Chirnside and Dickson away in full dress. Got a snackie frae Simpson when he came for his byke. Some socks [came] frae Jeanie for the laddies.

Saturday 10 October 1914

Meeting of police at 4.30 – Inspector Chrissie, Dickson, Cockburn, old Bob from the Knowes. Lachie down from Haddington. Sent a message for me. Miss Ogilvie [and] Mr William Burn
driving out with McLeod. Miss Maud and Suzie Curr in great
style. Old Mrs Ho-Ho not to be seen.

Sunday 11 October 1914

Very quiet day. Lay about all day. J Storey and Dr Black driving
about all day, always when the Kirk is in.

Monday 12 October 1914

Tam Hume, gaffer in the absence of Denholm, and son, Murray,
and Cockburn at 5.00 p.m. Very quiet day here.

Tuesday 13 October 1914

Wet day. Mickie's at East Linton, boozing. Mr White drove
away two hundred boll of crop to East Linton Station.

Wednesday 14 October

George Chirnside awa to Kirkland Hill seekin money. Cockburn
at 11.00 a.m. No-one turned up.

Thursday 15 October 1914

George Chirnside Taking signature. Bella and I at tattie lifting.
Gave a driver a flower en-passant.

Friday 16 October 1914

Bald's dog run over by Peter Clark CL.

Saturday 17 October 1914

Willie home for a week and looks very fresh.

Sunday 18 October 1914

Lay about all day. Lachie never got down last night. Willie
went home by the last train.

Monday 19 October 1914

Sale day at Linton. Meeting [of] police at 10.30.

Tuesday 20 October 1914

Wrote asking a day off. War news very good. Wrote also to
Sandy. His birthday on Thursday.

Wed 21 October 1914

Very quiet day. No bobbies. Howmuir driving away corn.
J Jamson and Jock Donald ill.

Thursday 22 October 1914

George Chirnside at midday Taking Signature. Dickson and J
Cockburn at 8.30 p.m. Letter from Sandy. He has been at Manchester Infirmary with Alick getting tonsels cut out of his throat.
No word of Willie coming home. Bob saw Tammy Sanderson
last night in Linton. Malcolm and Alick McDonald at home.
Clark Maideu and W Miller up the brae. Chirnside took his
bottle away.

Friday 23 October 1914

No sign of Willie yet. Alick and Malk [Malcolm] McDonald at
home. Inoculated for Eterick[66]

Saturday 24 October 1914

Lachie down for a clean sark. Police at 10.30. Chirnside and
Cockburn and Dickson.

Sunday 25 October 1914

Lay about all day after I got the newspaper. Jamie down from
Haddington. No sign of Willie. Police at 3.30 p.m. Chirsie
[Chirnside], Cockburn and Dickson. Had a call off Mrs Stenhouse – cab from Dunbar. Went up the brae at 11.00 p.m. and
came down at 1.00 a.m. Jim up with a half-drunk [...].

Monday 26 October 1914

Sale day at Linton. Saw Anthony Gray passing with Andrew Blyth. Saw George Chirnside and gave him a letter he lost in my cabin. Saw Mrs J McLeod going down on her byke. She'd an awfull red face wi the exertion. No good news frae the war. Wonder how poor Angus will be getting on, if alive.

Tuesday 27 October 1914

Letter from Willie for clothes. Sent them up per parcel post. Saw a lot of moving lights over East Linton. Mr and Mrs White driving out – last of his crop away. Linesman at 3:30.

Wed 28 October 1914

Masher[67] from Dunbar en route for Tynninghame to see Auld George Bailie. George Chirnside at 5.00 p.m. Campbell awa to Whitekirk wi Peter Clark. C L surfacemen all got a pair of rabbits from Biel.

Thursday 29 October

My left foot so bad [I] had to take off my boot and put on a shoe. George Cockburn passing in the dark. J Denholm getting his snares lifted, rabbit and all, for nought.

Friday 30 October 1914

Wrote reminding the superintendent of my application for a day off. Also to Nell in answer to hers. Cockburn going to Dunbar. Old J Logie coming in his place at Whitekirk. No word from Poor Angus. Wilson's dog howling in the field. Mr White got 64£ for one of his horses from Mr McIntyre. No byke. Donald driving him to and from market. My ankle very sore.

Saturday 31 October 1914

Willie here to get over his vaccination for fever. He was done at Edinburgh, and came home on [the] last train last night.

Sunday 1 November 1914
Lay about all day. So did the boys.

Monday 2 November 1914
So Lachie has gone with the Royal Scots to France. Poor Lachie, he would not take a telling so he is in God's hands and must take his chance. His mother is in a state about him.

Tuesday 3 November 1914
Letter from Nell. All well. Been a very quiet day here. Got a letter from Angus. He is alright, he says 'in the pink', and enjoying himself. Poor chap. I hope God will protect him and send him home victorious through all this murderous war.

Wednesday 4 November 1914
Went to Mrs Thompson's funeral. Got a ride home in Curr's car. Jamie came doon with Lachie's byke and went up in the train. Bob Dickson and Murray at 8.00 p.m. Logie did not turn up.

Thursday 5 November
Letter from Lachie, from Southampton.

Friday 6 November 1914
Bella at Haddington getting her Divide.[68]

Saturday 7 November 1914
Postcard from Lachie. He has got over the jab and is well. Letter from Uncle Roderick. They are all well. Full meet of Police at 4.30. J Logie arrove at White Kirk. No word of any leave for me from old Black.

Sunday 8 November 1914
Bob at Church. Sogers kirked.[69] Chaplain officiating, along with old Tomie.

Monday 9 November 1914

Very quiet day. No one going about. Bob Gutherston here last night and Bella washing.

Tuesday 10 November 1914

Letter from Jean and Aunt Nell. Both well. The notorious *Emden* sunk by an Australian, The *Kharbrush*[70] blocked and bombarded. Good Riddiance Both.

Wed 11 November 1914

Big wedding at Edinburgh. James and Miss Stewart away in company.

Thursday 12 November 1914

Postcard from Lachie. He is well, he says. Bella at Portobello. George Chirnside at 2.35, Taking Signature. [He] says the 8th Royal Scots are in the firing line already. Poor Lachie is soon in. It's only two months listed. Jean is well and sent me some tobacco.

Friday 13 November 1914

Very quiet day. Nothing doing. Just wondering about Lachie.

Saturday 14 November 1914

George Chirnside, Logie and Dickson at 4.30. Old Bob and George Colston. Willie home with his innoculation again. Brought home a dispatch with a paragraph from Lithgow saying Angus was killed on the 26th October. Poor Angus. I always thought yon was the last we would see of him when he waved out of the fast [train]. May God recieve his soul.

Sunday 15 November 1914

Sad day with us all. Willie and Bob at the Kirk. The Minister mentioned Angus' reported death from the pulpit. John Logie and his wife at 5.00 p.m. – very wet.

Monday 16 November 1914

Letter from George. He is well. Also D Ramage [nephew]. He was sympathising with us and expressing his sorrow about Angus. Had to send a wire after Willie to come home at once as all leave was stopped.

Tuesday 17 [Nov]ember 1914

Letters from Sandy, George and Jean. Sandy's wife is ill – has fallen down the stair and hurt her knee. Poor Lizzie. George wants to hear about Angus, but it's no use now. Jean would like to come home but that also is no use just now. Bob Sanderson saw Willie at Haddington today, so he is all right so far. I wrote to Sandy, and Bella is writing to Jeanie.

Wednesday 18 November 1914

Letters from Willie, Aunt Nell and Lizzie. No news of Angus yet. Hales working at Linton. Wrote to Davie and his mother.

Thursday 19 November 1914

Old Tennant here with a letter from headquarters saying for him to try and send one of his own men to relieve me, but I told him the time was past. I could have told him a lot more, but refrained.

Friday 20 November 1914

No word of Angus. Poor Angus. I wish I knew. And Poor Lachie. We have a postcard from [him]. He is well and sticking it out, but no number yet.

Saturday 21 November 1914

Jeanie arrove from Edinburgh per 2:1 train. She is looking pretty well and brought a portrait of Uncle Roderick. Written in the darkening last night.

Sunday 22 November 1914

Mr Marchbanks called. Jean was away to the Free Kirk so she

didna see him. Been thinking of Lachie all day and waiting to hear about Angus. It's weary waiting. Police here at 4:30.

Monday 23 November 1914

All police except Campbell at 4.30. Jean went away home by the last train. Bob went in with [her]. No word from War Office. Aunt Nell and Sandy wrote.

Tuesday 24 November

No word of Angus yet. Hear that Lachie's regiment has been fighting on the eighteenth.

Wednesday 25 November 1914

A month since Angus wrote his last letter home and no word yet.

Thursday 26 November 1914

Chirnside here and Miss Innes and Miss Ogilvie. Some of the men of Lachie's regiment killed and wounded. His mother is in a sad state of fear.

Friday 27 November 1914

Bella McKinlay up. She also is anxious about her son, George. We can't keep our spirits up. Thinking about Lachie, poor man, so God be with him.

Saturday 28 November 1914

Willie down for the weekend. Jamie D on the road. Got some notices about troop trains coming on Monday. No word of Angus. George Chirnside has got a letter from Tom, and the boys were all right on the twenty second.

Sunday 29 November 1914

Went to the Post Office but no word from, or of, Angus or Lachie so we are very sad today. Willie went away by the last train too. He seems depressed too.

Monday 30 November 1914

Letter from Aunt Nell. Bob Dickson down for his pay, also T. McIntosh, Donald and Howmuir. Hinds down wi their new carts and horses. Had a crack with Miss Innes. Bob away for a paper. Tramp making marks on the dyke.

Tuesday 1 December 1914

No word from Lachie, poor chap. Hope he is in the land of the living, said Miss Innes.

Wednesday 2 December 1914

George Chirnside taking signature. Howmuir took up 50 bullocks. James Craig helped him along with them. Mrs Ogilvie [is] going to send Lachie a Christmas present – so sent [her] his address.

Thursday 3 December 1914

Have written away to the War Office for news of Angus, if they have any. John Logie and Dickson at 11.00 a.m. Chirnside at 4.15 p.m. Very wet night turned after a gale of wind south-west. Georgina and the doctor awa up.

Friday 4 December 1914

No word yet of Angus. Letter[s] from D Ramage and Kennith McLean. No word of Lachie yet. It's a weary wait, but we're all in God's hands and must submit. In His own good time we'll know all.

Saturday 5 December 1914

Wrote to Colonel Brook asking about Lachie, also to Aunt Nell. Mrs and Miss Ogilvey of Biel calling on Bella. John Logie Dickson and Murray at 4.30 p.m. Tam Hume, on the road, put out the East Distant lamp for me and it's out, I see.

Sunday 6 December 1914

Very quiet day. Lay about all day. Letter from Sandy – Lizzie getting some better.

Monday 7 December 1914

No word about Angus, but a letter from Lachie. He is well, so I sent him off a postcard saying we were glad to hear from him. Wrote also to Aunt Lizzie, Rorie and D Ramage.

Tuesday 8 December 1914

Logie at 10.30. Mrs Stenhouse with Lachie's helmet and so we have all we need for his Christmas parcel. Will have to write to George and Andrew.

Wednesday 9 December 1914

Bella went into M Innes but too late, so posted Lachie's parcel.

Thursday 10 December 1914

No word from War Office so poor Angus must be lost. George Chirnside here taking signatures. Told him about signalling on Pencraig and at Tyninghame House

Friday 11 December 1914

Chirnside at 11.00 a.m. came down the brae. New sow barrow for Howmuir – gettin them in good time. Postcard from Lachie. He is well and wanting chocolates. Bob Dickson at 5.00 p.m. John Logie didn't turn up.

Saturday 12 December 1914

Chirnside at 10.00 a.m. Adam Johnston on the road. Alick Jamson calling en passant. They had a kirn[71] last night so they got a day off. No letters today. Military Special at 4.40. Horse boxes. Bob put one lamp only. Maggie King away up to see her sister. Howmuir plooing [ploughing].

Sunday 13 December 1914
Here all day.

Monday 14 December 1914

Sent away papers to Canada, and letters to Sandy and Aunt
Nell. Police at 10.30 – Murray, Logie and Dickson. Sale at East
Linton pit shed [...]. Stewart's here, having Jim with him. Jamie
looking for the inspector, who never came.

Tuesday 15 December 1914

Saw Miss Innes. Signalling going on on Pencraig Hill about six
o'clock. Stop[p]ed abruptly. Some one trying on his hand in the
Tyninghame grounds. Half an hour later two lights waved
violently in East Linton and one on [the] Lawhead road. Also
motor at Tyninghame Dam Brig. Tam and his men busy all day.
Got a telegram form from station. Military train at 10.45 from
the south. Mr Marjoribanks carriage down at six o'clock train.
Stone engin[e]s driving all day from the law, two runs each way.
Miss Ogilvie and Curtis left for the 11.15 train. McLeod with
c[arriage] and pair.

Wednesday 16 December 1914
Washing day. Wet and dirty. Cleared up towards evening.

Thursday 17 December 1914

Mrs Stenhouse with Bella in the evening. John Logie at 8.30
p.m. German raid on Hartlepool and Scarborough.

Friday 18 December 1914

Bugler here blowing and a dog howling back. News soon. Logie
and Dickson here. Lot of light signallers at Linton.

Saturday 19 December 1914

Angus killed in battle on the 26th October 1914. Poor Angus.
May God recieve his soul in Heaven.[72]

Sunday 20 December 1914

Meet of police at 3.30. Chirnside, Logie and Dickson. Wrote a lot of letters to all our friends about Angus' death. Jamie down from Haddington. He looks quite fresh.

Monday 21 December 1914

Went to Dunbar and saw Registrar. He could not do anything as Angus did not die in Parish. Called on Society man and got home in good time. Linesman sorting signals – oiling frame, etc.

Tuesday 22 December 1914

Very quiet day. Bella washing James' clothes.

Wed 23 December 1914

Letters and cards of sympathy from A Bowhill, Miss Lyle and John D Hope, Haddington. So I'll have to acknowledge the same next week – God willing.

Thursday 24 December 1914

Lady Frances Balfour[73] here with an Christmas present for Bella and I. She is the only kind lady among all the aristocrats about here. Got ten cwt of coal from Henry Lunem. Bob brought them along, 10/6. Our own Bob is going to pay for them as a Christmas present.

Friday 25 December 1914

Christmas day very quiet this year. Tyninghame folks all up as usual. Willie here from Haddington. Got a postcard from Lachie. He is well, he says, and got my letter, etc. Poor Lach, he is soon in the strife. May God protect him.

Saturday 26 December 1914

Two months have gone since poor Angus was killed and we [have now] got the Society money, 10£ for his loss. I would rather have seen his honest face come in at the door than all the

money in the banks. Letter from Uncle Roderick. Old John
Rose on the road.

Sunday 27 December 1914
Very quiet day. Stayed at home and wrote some letters.

Monday 28 December 1914
Got a nice letter from Dr Marjoribanks of Stenton and saw
and thanked him at night en passant.

Tuesday 29 December 1914
Letter from Lachie. Poor chap, he is suffering six days in
trenches without a sleep. Also from William Kinnear from
Alexandra. Sending awa Lachie's New Year.

Wed 30 December 1914 –

Thur 31 December 1914
Bob got the sack from Cowie so it's questionable where he may
land. Very quiet night. No sign of New Year. Hope we may have
a much better year, 1915. Just one hundred years since Water-
loo was fought in Belgium.

Friday 1 January 1915
New Year's day. Not much work going on here. All busy drinking as usual. Jamie down from Haddington and brought me
some gifts. Young Tam Denholm and Tam Hume away for a
weekend.

Saturday 2 January 1915
Willie down with a dram for me. Meet of police at 3.30 p.m. –
all but Inspector Campbell. No word from Lachie. Hope he has
got his New Year's parcel. Tamson (farmer) plooin [ploughing]
his self. Donald awa weekend.

Sunday 3 January 1915

Bob went to church. I stayed at home.

Monday 4 January 1915

Young Tam not out of it. Men all working out there. Road roller not working. Bob not working yet.

Tuesday 5 January 1915

Wrote a lot of letters but missed the post twice. Bob at Balancrieff and at Haddington. He got a promised start tomorrow but did not think much of it, so won't go to it.

Wednesday 6 January 1915

Bob got a start at Haddington, with Orr, so sent up his tools with the Streets train. Wrote to W J Kinnear and Uncle Roderick.

Thursday 7 January 1915

Bob started at the yeomanry camps at Annesfield Park. Block at Dunbar. Railway policeman en route for Beltonford. Some Barley [has] gone a missing. Sandy Nimmold on a goods train.

Friday 8 January 1915

Official notice from The War Office, schedule A. They are looking after his personal effects [and] back pay and so I will not need to write yet awhile. Poor Angus, I thought always I'd seen the last of him passing.

Friday 8 January 1915

Sent away a box of eggs to Jean per post.

Saturday 9 January 1915

Letter from Captain Stirling, Territorial SCO, Haddington. Lachie is sending some money to his mother. Got an awful fright – thought something was wrong. His mother was nearly fainting. Very quiet day here. Bob put out my lamps at 11.00 p.m. Bobbies at North Lodge.

Sunday 10 January 1915
Bella at the Kirk. Bella and I had a long crack. Bob away at night.

Monday 11 January 1915
Lewis trotted past and never spoke. Linesman oiling my gate and frame. Miss Innes calling. Bella at Post Office – got 8/6 from Lachie. Logie, Murray and Dickson at 10.00 a.m.

Tuesday 12 January 1915
Bob Dickson at 10.30. Letter from Lachie. He is bad with his feet again – been standing in wet trenches for five days, but not so badly off as some of his mates. Got my notice to send in my b[ank] book to Mr Laing, Edinburgh.

Wednesday 13 January 1915
Bob Dickson, J Logie and Murray – Bellhaven at 8.00 p.m. Wrote a letter to Lachie. Poor Lach, has sore feet and [is] a bit down-hearted.

Thursday 14 January 1915
Logie and Chirnside at 11.30 a.m. Road Guides here inter-cepting dispatch carriers from Haddington. Nelson Pleasants stationed here. Sent away my bank book to Mr Laing. Sent away a parcel letter to Lachie. Hope it's God's will he may get them – to cheer him up [and] to let him see we are always think-ing of him. Letter from Mary Forsythe from Drem, Newmains. [She] wants Bella to come and see her mother on Sunday first. Banish [the] sight.

Friday 15 January 1915
Willie arrove for a weekend. Very quiet day. Hope poor Lachie

is still to the fore. There has been stiff fighting at La Bàssee, near where he is lying.

Saturday 16 January 1915

Willie knocking about and at Linton all night, but came home alright. Had a call off Seargeant Main who brought me a dram. He is from Tranent and is Pay Seargent for the National Reserve.

Sunday 17 January 1915

Jamie [here] from Haddington. He is looking very well. Willie here also – and well.

Monday 18 January 1915

Letter from Nell and Jean, both well. Inspector Campbell and Murray at 4.30. Seargent from Seacliff [North Berwick] – en passant.

Tuesday 19 January 1915

Great fire at Biel Grange. Big squads coming and going – cycles and motors. Bob was up till ten o'clock. Old Curr, Coltart and Johnston head Police action – impudent puppies.

Wednesday 20 January 1915

Letter from Lachie. He is in hospital with a burnt eye done by a spark of boiling grease out of a frying pan. Hope it won't spoil his eyesight. Poor chap. May God protect and bring him safe home to his mother. Bess Knowes driving away tatties to Beltonford Station.

Thursday 21 January 1915

Wrote to Aunt Nell, so if Jean is down she'll get the news from home. George Blaikie says he's not going back to the Front again, but I doot [that].

Friday 22 January 1915

Bob Dickson and J Logie at 5.00 p.m. George [McKenzie] and C Smith at Haddington getting their [...]. No word from anyone.

Saturday 23 January 1915

T Denholm on the road. No word from Jean this week, or Sandy either, so hope they are both well.

Sunday 24 January 1915

Trains blocked at Berwick. N E couldn't take them away. Naval battle in the North Sea. Stephen Ramage [nephew] en passant to Birnieknows and the Mains.

Monday 25 January 1915

Meet of police at 10.30. G Chirnside, Logie and Dickson. Inspector Campbell passing. Bob Dickson down for pay.

Tuesday 26 January 1915

No word from Lachie. We are wearying to hear from him again.

Wed 27 January 1915

Great naval battle on Sunday in [the] North Sea. [The] Germans got [...] and run home when ever they saw our ships. Blücher sunk, and some smaller craft.[74]

Thursday 28 January 1915

Chirnside and Logie here, and at Dunbar on business. No word from Lachie. Letter from one of his mates.

Friday 29 January 1915

Letter from Lachie. He is in hospital at Boulogne – temperature high and he is keept in bed with some throat and chest complication as well as his eye – which is getting better, he says. Poor soul, but we were very pleased to hear from him and hope he may mend now. If its God's will and pleasure to send him home, we will be very glad to see him again.

Saturday 30 January 1915

Meet of police at 4.00 p.m. All but [the] inspector. No word from anybody. John Rose on the road.

Sunday 31 January 1915

Mrs and Mr T_ and three ladies from Tyninghame House at Biel Chapel. Bella filled up her paper for Territorial Association but has to get it signed. Dr Wedderburn is leaving on Thursday, bidding me good-bye.

Monday 1 February 1915

Chirnside signed the wife's paper and I sent it away to Haddington. Letter from Sandy. They are all well. Very quiet day. Bob very tired. Submarines at work in the Irish Sea – sunk three ships and took off the crew.

Thursday 4 March 1915

After many days I am getting better.

Monday 8 March 1915

Am still in the land of the living, and the place of hope. Not very strong yet but can't complain as I might be worse. Painters here making dirt – eight or nine of them. Lachie [now back from France] away to Haddington for his byke, which Bill took away on Saturday night.

Monday 15 March 1915

Another week passed and a man appointed as my successor from Burnmouth. He is a surfaceman at present. Old Tennant down yesterday. They are asking if the house is empty yet. I walked in and saw the doctor and got my bottle filled. I was

1. Dodridge Farm, Ormiston, where Andrew was born in 1854.

2. Myles Farm, where the family moved to from Dodridge.

3. Harrow Hotel, Dalkeith.

4. Ecclaw Farm, of which Andrew said he was 'grieved to [go] where there was nothing to view but whins and heather and bleak mountains'.

5.

5. Clints Farm, where Andrew went as a groom after leaving home for the first time.

6. Cockpen, where Andrew's mother was laid to rest.

7. Shepherd's cottage at Kidshielhaugh Farm. Andrew worked here for a term before heading off to live with his sister, Jane.

6.

7.

8. Andrew's sister, Mary, and her family, Ettrick, 1883.

9. Helen (Nell) Robertson (Andrew's sister-in-law).

10. Andrew's brother, James, with his family, 1887.

11.

11. Newspaper advertisement seeking information about Andrew's brother, William. *Montreal Witness*, 1889.

12. Andrew and boy at Biel Gate, c.1905.

13. Andrew, Bella and family at Biel Gate, c.1920.

14. Mary and Roderick MacLean, c.1900, Andrew's sister and brother-in-law.

15. Agnes McLaren, Andrew's sister, with Elizabeth (Colina) and Mary, her daughters.

16. Alexander (son, Sandy) and his family, Cheshire, *c.*1910.

17. Alexander, at post as a chauffeur, Cheshire, *c.*1910.

18. Alexander and Robert (son, Bob), *c.*1910.

19. Andrew (son) in Canada, *c.*1910.

20 (a–d.) (opposite) Pages of a letter and envelope from Andrew to his son, Andrew, in Canada.

20 a.

Craigie Cottage
Cramond Bridge.
Edinburgh
Scotland
12/4/15

Dear Andrew

His is my new
address we arrove here on the 1st
day of april + have got fairly
settled down I have taken the house
till martinmas at £15 per annum so we
have left the gates after 30 years of
storm & stress being fairly happy
most of the time the worry about
Angus.s death fairly knocked
me up + now I am useless for work

b.

We have Willie + Jackie here for
a week out from Haddington
they are both well . I think Poor
Jack is bound for France again
they have been inoculating him
against Fever So that is a sign
but they never tell them anything
Jean was with us for 10 days
helping her mother + Bob as
head man for four So I had
nothing to do. Your mother
has had a busy fortnight and has
got everything ship shape I hope
you are keeping in good
health and getting on with

c.

your Sowing we have had
a pretty cold spring here
but not much snow this
is a later district by about
3 weeks here than E Lothian
No news from Geo for a long
time So I am writing him sup-
hur adress for your Uncle Rob
and aunt Nell have both been
down with Bronchitis Bob has
got the Sack from the Mill
Sorry So I dont know what will
come over him after being so
long driving horses

d.

we get a grand view of the
Forth Bridge here + the Fleet
lying in the Firth of Forth
Waiting for the Germans to
come up + fight them . So now
Dear Andrew with Kindest
love from us Both I remain
Your loving Father
Andrew Ramage .

Mr Andrew Ramage
Melaval . Sask .
Canada .

RETIRAL OF A RAILWAY SERVANT. — Mr Andrew Ramage, who, for about thirty years, has been gatekeeper at Biel railway crossing, has retired from the service of the North British Railway Company, owing to the state of his health. His calling brought him in contact with a great many people, among one and all of whom he won for himself golden opinions by reason of his unfailing courtesy and kindness.

22.

23.

Biel Gate
Prestonkirk
aug 6th 1914

Dear Jeanie
This is a sad time with us here Just now with the Boys going away and all this talk of war. Angus went past Yesterday at midday for London Poor Chap who knows but It may be our last view of Him It fairly knocked Your Mother up but she is composed & resigned to the will of God who knows what is best. Willie is at Dunbar but I hear they are going to York to relieve the Scots Greys we are all well here at Present Uncle Rottie is staying with us for a day or two he was in seeing Flo on Tuesday, Jujie is coming for Ella next week I wish she was away as she is nervous about all this talk of War so as this is all my news I will conclude with kindest love to you from us all while I remain your loving Father
Andw Ramage

24.

21. Andrew, 1913.

22. Retiral newspaper notice, 1915.

23. Letter from Andrew to his daughter, Jean, 6 August 1914.

24. Andrew and his wife, Bella, at Biel Gate, close to his retirement, c.1914.

SOME. O THE LADDIES

THE MERRY JOCKS

POST CARD

CARTE POSTALE—POSTKARTE

Communication—Mittellung—Correspondance.   Address—Adresse—Afrese

Hope this finds you all as it
leaves me in the best of health
and spirits I suppose Willie
will be having a great time
with his crush this year so
far from home, got Fathers letter
all right shall write when I
get time thats all this time

Mrs Andrew Ramage
Biel Rly Gates
Prestonkirk
Scotland

25 (a–b.) Postcard
home from Angus
(son), Scots Guards,
Caterham, 1910.
(Angus is in the second
row, second in from
the left).

26. Angus, Linlithgow
Police, 1913. (Angus is
on the right.)

27.

No 7637 Pte A Ramage
L F boy 2 Scots Gds
20th Inf Brigade
Lyndhurst Camp
Hants England

Dear Dad,
I received your welcome letter the day we left the Tower (about ten days ago) & was pleased to see that you were all well etc. We are down here at this place, which is about ten miles from S Hampton going through about as rough a bit of training as any man can stick. We dont know when we will sail, but have to be prepared to shift at any moment. I expect we will be off before the end of next week. We have been waiting on the 2d Gordons from Cairo the same mob that relieved us out there. They arrived here last night so no doubt we will soon be out of it & into the thick of the scrap. I am in the pink myself & just wearying to get away as marching for days & digging trenches here, where it was required gets on my nerves. Thats about all there is to say at present or will close with kindest love to all while I remain your Affect son Angus Ramage

28 a.

SS Lesbaun
Soth Hampton

Dear Father & Mother
It has come at last & we are on board ready for the road. We expect to sail this afternoon about 5 PM. so we wont be long now before we see something of the Germans. We have no idea where we will land & when we do I wont be able to let you know

but if you hear anything of the 7th Div you will know I am there. We marched down here from Lyndhurst last night (its about ten miles) .... proper, there is eight of them going with this lot so you may .... there is a good few troops.

b. I have no more

to say so I will say so long & wish you the best of health etc until I return. Cheerio the toffs well meantime I remain your Affect son Angus Ramage

P.S. No 7637 .... L F boy 2 Scots ...... 20 Inf Brigade British Expeditionary ......

c.

27. Letter from Angus, September 1914.

28 (a–c.) Letter from Angus, October 1914.

29. Letter from the Scots Guards advising Andrew of the death of Angus on 26 October 1914.

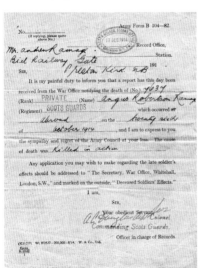

Army Form B 104—82
No. _____
(If replying, please quote above No.)

Record Office,
_____ Station.

Mr Andrew Ramage
Birl Railway Gate
Preston Kirk NB

_____ 191 .

SIR,

It is my painful duty to inform you that a report has this day been received from the War Office notifying the death of (No.) 7637 (Rank) PRIVATE (Name) Angus Robertson Ramage (Regiment) SCOTS GUARDS which occurred at Abroad on the twenty sixth of October 1914, and I am to express to you the sympathy and regret of the Army Council at your loss. The cause of death was Killed in action.

Any application you may wish to make regarding the late soldier's effects should be addressed to "The Secretary, War Office, Whitehall, London, S.W.," and marked on the outside, "Deceased Soldiers' Effects."

I am,

SIR,

Your obedient Servant,
_____ Colonel
Commanding Scots Guards.

Officer in charge of Records.

29.

30. Roll Call of Angus's battalion (2nd Battalion, Scots Guards) at Ypres on the morning of 27 October 1914 – the day after Angus was Killed in Action.

31. (a–b.) Condolence letter following Angus' death, from Rev. Marjoribanks of Stenton Church, dated 26 December 1914.

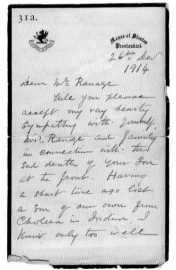

31a.

Manse of Stenton
Prestonkirk
26th Dec
1914

Dear Mr Ranage

Will you please accept my very hearty sympathy with yourself, Mrs Ranage and family in connection with the sad death of your son at the front. Having a short time ago lost a son of our own from Cholera in India, I know only too well

what your feelings at the present time must be. We here are trying to take comfort in the thought that Christmas time tells us the great truth of God's coming to the help of man at the very time of man's greatest need of God "with boldness therefore at the Throne. Let us make all our sorrows known and ask the aid of heavenly power, To help us in the evil hour."

Mrs Marjoribanks joins with me in heartfelt sympathy

Yours very faithfully
Fe Marjoribanks

b.

32.

32. William (son, Bill) with Territorial Army, 1909. (Bill is second from the right, back.)

33 (a–b.) Postcard from Bill to his sister, Jean. Lothian and Borders Horse, Haddington, August 1914. (Bill is the fifth seated person in from the right.)

34. Bill in army uniform, Edinburgh, 1916.

33 a.

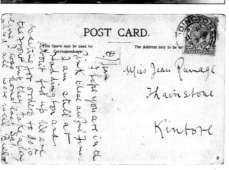

34.

b.

35. Robert (son, Bob) with Fraser's Squad, McArthur's Joiners, East Linton, 1912. (Bob is second from the left.)

36. Bob, RFC, 1915 (Bob is the second from the left, front).

37. Bob, RFC, 1916. (Bob is first on the left, back).

38. Bob, RFC, 1916.

36.

37.   ROWNER

38.

39. James (son, Jim), Military Mounted Police Christmas Dinner, 1915. (Jim is in the centre, under the window.)

40. Jim (front right), Military Mounted Police, around 1916.

41. Jim (extreme right), *c.*1917.

42. Jim, Military Mounted Police, *c.*1918.

43. Jim, Military Mounted Police,
Roustchouk, Bulgaria, February 1919.

45. Lauchlan (son, Lachie) in Royal
Scots Uniform, with sister, Jean, c.1914.

44. W A Ramage (Billie, nephew: back,
left), Canadian Expeditionary Force,
1916.

46. Lachie (first on right), Royal Scots,
1917.

47.

48.

49.

50.

47. Lachie, Royal Scots, c.1917.
(Lachie is first left, rear.)

48. (Left to right) Alexander
(Sandy), Lauchlan (Lachie),
Elizabeth (Ella) and Elizabeth
(Lizzie), c.1918.

49. Lachie, Royal Scots, and
Robert (Bob), RAF, c.1919.

50. Family memorial at
Prestonkirk.

very tired when I got home. Lachie away to Peebles again. He does not expect to get home this time. Another letter from The War office to see about Angus' will. Damn them and their will and letters both.

Tuesday 16 March 1915

Took a walk down to Tyninghame village. [This] brought back sad memories so I came home as soon as I could. Would not like to stay there now. God knows where will I land yet. Turned out all my old iron and bicycle tyres for Broadly. Got a bed of chaff from Pat McKinlay, so we are right for a fresh bed. Wind away into the east, and very cold. No letters. Bella away to Gateside for her money.

Wednesday 17 March 1915

Very stormy day – snow and sleet. Lay in bed all day.

Thursday 18 March 1915

Bella at Linton, seeing about a house. But no luck – it's taken already, and not a good house.

Friday 19 March 1915

Met Miss Innes coming out to tell us about another house. She is very kind. Saw old Ho-Ho about the insurance and he is going to write to Short. Had a bad turn after I came home. Had Mrs Stenhouse.

Saturday 20 March 1915

Went to Linton and saw old Ho-Ho. I am to go to Edinburgh and see a doctor of repute, so I said I'd go on Tuesday. Came home with Willie and George Chirnside. Willie went off to Edinburgh later.

Sunday 21 March 1915

Jean's birthday. Thirty years [old] now, poor lassie. No word of Lachie. I was three times at Howmuir road and walking. Had

George Chirnside. He has been at Bill Middlemass and he could give us a house till the term.[75]

Monday 22 March 1915

Saw old Ho-Ho. He is to give me tickets to Edinburgh for the wife and self [for] tomorrow.

Tuesday 23 March 1915

Went to Edinburgh and saw Doctor Sloan, Abercrombie Place, Edinburgh. He was very nice. Saw Jean and Aunt Nell. She and Bob [McLachlan, her husband] is very hard up. Both in bed, Thamie Green attending them. Got T Denholm to drive us home from last train.

Wed 24 March 1915

Very wet day. Stayed at home all day.

Thursday 26 March 1915

Went to the doctor but did not see him, so got my bottle filled. Saw old Ho-Ho but he has no word from Edinburgh yet.

Friday 26 March 1915

Letter from cousin Billie, John Jardine, and Jean. Billie is still in hospital. Jean was out at Craigie but David [nephew, a policeman at Dalmeny] has no word yet from the factor. Lachie and Jamie both here from Haddington – looking well. Sent away a letter to Young about my money. He's a twister.

Saturday 27 March 1915

Willie and L_ down from Haddington. Lachie did not turn up. No word from Davie yet.

Sunday 28 March 1915

Have got word about a house at Craigie So I must go to Edinburgh and see James Young about my S O money.

Monday 29 March 1915

Went to Edinburgh and saw James Young and got my money –
3£. Saw Mr Short […] He says I'll be all right with the S O and
can leave when I like, so arrange with Tennant to flit on
Wednesday.

Tuesday 30 March 1915

Got a lorry load of furniture away to station. Tam, Hume and
Denholm gave me a hand to load. Bob came down at night.

Wednesday 31 March 1915

Left Linton by 11.17 train after thirty years residence. Went and
saw Tam Marjoribanks and Mr and Mrs Chirnside and left
good friends with every one. Got to Dalmaney at 1.30 and here
at 6.00 p.m. Stayed with a neighbour, Mrs Muirhead, who
offered us a bed. Bob and Jean stayed with Davie.

Thursday 1 April 1915

No flitting. No furniture came. Day lost. All well. Jamie had to
go away home to work. Got word furniture came.

Friday 2 April 1915

Davie and Bob brought up all the furniture in three rakes. Very
wet, disagreeable day but got on all right.

Saturday 3 April 1915

Bob got the floor put right and had a very busy day and looked
tired when he went away down to Davie's to spend the evening.

Sunday 4 April 1915

Bob and Davie up from Dalmaney with the boys. Mrs Ramage
came up at night. She was pleased with the house. Spent a very
quiet day. Bob went away home to Haddington, and Jean went
to the station with him. Hope he does not loose his job over
being so long away.

Monday 5 April 1915

Took a walk to Cramond Bridge and saw the Postmistress and got a paper and brought up one for Miss Glendinning. Jean and her mother busy at house, cleaning. Had a good day myself. Never had a touch of my enemy. Davie up with a letter from Constable so will send his rent away tomorrow, God willing.

Tuesday 6 April 1915

Bella and Jean at Edinburgh and got home at 4.00 p.m. Very quiet day.

Wednesday 7 April 1915

Went to Queensferry and saw a new Panel[76] doctor and paid the van for bringing up the hens. Wish I had left them. Mr Constable writes and I'm either to shut them in or put them away.

Thursday 8 April 1915

Went to Craigie Hall and called on Mr Imrie. He was very nice and saw me off the ground. Went to Barnton and called at the station. No word of them yet. So we lost a chance. Lachie arrove at Dalmaney and Jean brought him home. Jamie went to the Ferry.

Friday 9 April 1915

Went to Edinburgh with Lachie and joined the St Cuthbert's Store[77] and paid in 50£ for Membership. Bought 7lb of mahogany stain in Bread Street. Paid 3/6 for paint, also 3/6 for my pen to Fairgreave, Cockburn Street. Alison Brownlee sorted my watch handles. They were only hawked. Got home at 2.30 p.m. Grand views out of the train. Jean left for Edinburgh at 5.30 p.m. from Barnton. Lachie took the byke and carried her bag for her. Willie arrove at 10.00 p.m. from Barnton. Came up with the station master to Craigiehall.

Saturday 10 April 1915

Saw old Henderson but he would not face up, only went to old Mary with her money. The boys at Dalmaney. I went down and saw Davie and Mrs Ramage. They are going to take my hens at 2/6 each, so that's the best way out of a bad job. Boys were planting taties when I came home. Lachie is not much worth, poor chap. They are over to the Ferry to see the sights so I [am] waiting on someone to come over and take the hens away. Perhaps Davie may come later.

Sunday 11 April 1915

Lachie and I took a walk to Dalmaney House and came up by the home farm and out at Barnbougle Lodge. He was about fed up walking. Willie stayed at home all day and took a rest and went off home at 5.30 p.m.

Monday 12 April 1915

Lachie went off home from Dalmaney Station. He has a sore toe. I went to the top of the hill and saw him away. It's too quiet here for him, but he says he likes the place. […]

Tuesday 13 April 1915

Went to Davidson's Mains store for bread and got up the bed from Barnton Station by one of Henderson's carts, which was lucky as I was going to hire a lorry to take it up. Got a letter from Sandy. His wife is come better, he says, and able to do her work. Planted three rows of potatoes in the afternoon. Craigie folks busy plantin tatties. The twa lassies both working. No word about the store drawman starting work yet.

Wednesday 14 April 1915

Big day painting and took a walk to Queensferry and got my bottle filled, and made some other purchases.

Thursday 15 April 1915

Had a big day painting and took a walk to Kirkliston – two miles. Was very tired when I got home. Didn't see Mr Bowmaker.

Friday 16 April 1915

Painting some more. Took a walk to Dalmaney and saw David busy with his hens. Came home a new road and cut up some stick. Mr and Mrs Irvine up shaking hands with Mrs Muirhead.

Saturday 17 April 1915

Went to Edinburgh and Portobello. Got my Guard's money and made some purchases. Uncle Rob is never working yet, but both keeping stronger. Adam was out working. Got a letter from Mr Short saying I had got the Superannuation Allowance of 1£ per week from the North British Railway Company after forty years service. Bob arrove from Haddington at 8.00 p.m. He came to Leith and Granton Road from Portobello and took a long time. But he had a strong head wind all the way.

Sunday 18 April 1915

Bob and I took a walk round by Dalmaney and Dolphington. He had a big day mending the water pipe. He left at 3.00 p.m en route for Hoprigg Mains [East Lothian]. Davie's two laddies – Erick and Daw – came over to say their mother would be here on Thursday if Jean was coming from Edinburgh.

Monday 19 April 1915

Busy day painting. Went to the Ferry and met D Ramage and turned and came home by Dalmaney and had a stiff climb up the Craigie Hill. Miss Muirhead had a holiday and was walking out [with] her lad.

Tuesday 20 April 1915

Busy day in the garden and carrying sticks, but never left the old shebang.

Wednesday 21 April 1915

Painting and carrying sticks. No letters from anyone.

Thursday 2 April 1915 – Took a rest all day. No letters.

Friday 23 April 1915

Went to Jones' sale at Dalmeny and bought a bed, a night stool or commode, a carpet, some pictures and a bed rest for £1 14s 6d, 3s for a hire and 1s for the boys.

Saturday 24 April 1915

Got a letter from Jean. She is some better but not up yet. She has had a letter from cousin Billie [Canada]. Got my National Insurance money all right and wrote Woods and Short. Sowed a drill of sweet peas and carried home some firewood. No word from any of the boys. Yeomanry bound for Hedderwick Camp early in May. Advanced party there already making preparation for [the] regiment coming. Fifty five of 8th Royal Scots under orders for the Front, to make good the wastage.

Sunday 25 April 1915

Bella and I took [a] run down to the sea by the Dalmeny home farm and got a nice walk. Rows about milk with the girl.

Monday 26 April 1915

Went to Edinburgh and bought paper and paint for the kitchen. Got a letter from Bob and Lachie and Aunt Nell.

Tuesday 27 April 1915

Had a great day papering the kitchen and got it finished, but hardly enough paper.

Wednesday 28 April 1915

Took a run to Dalmeny. All well there. Another letter from War Office about Angus' will etc.

Thursday 29 April 1915

Jean here from Edinburgh and took away her byke. She has got a shake. Sent away letter to War Office.

Friday 30 April 1915

Went to the Ferry and saw Doctor Dickson and bought some fish and came home. Carried and broke sticks. Letter from Short, and postcard from Lachie.

Saturday 1 May 1915

No Insurance money. Had a bad day. Cold east wind.

Sunday 2 May 1915

Went up the hill to view the north hills. Grampians covered with snow. Took a bad turn and had to run down again. Met Jean on the road, with Mr Hall.

Monday 3 May 1915

No National Insurance money yet. Wonder what's up. Had a bad turn and a big day, working and carrying sticks and breaking them up.

Tuesday 4 May 1915

No money yet. Wrote away and sent the Doctor's Certificate. Went down to Dalmeny and saw Mrs R. David came up to Bonniton with me and got me some putty to mend the water pipe. So I made a start as soon as I got home.

Wednesday 5 May 1915

Went to Haddington and saw Willie, Jamie and Lachie. Gave Lachie 6s from his mother. Settled with the Store. Got 6£. Jamie and I dined at the George [Haddington]. Jamie came to Portobello and Edinburgh with us and saw us into the train for Barnton.

Thursday 6 May 1915

Walked to Turnhouse Station. Saw young Login who has got the appointment of Station Manager. Felt very tired with the long walk.

Friday 7 May 1915

Painting all day. Had Davie calling in the evening.

Saturday 8 May 1915

Painting all day. Nearly walked to the Ferry and got a *Scotsman* to see about the sinking of the S S *Lucitania* near Old [Head of] Kinsail, in Ireland, by a submarine. Horror of the whole world. No sign of any of the boys. Got a rabbit from James Darling as I came home.

Sunday 9 May 1915

Bella and I took a walk to Burnshot and came home by the Barnbougle Lodge. Not so many sailors flying past in motors. Davie's boys here at tea – Erick and David. Very quiet day.

Monday 10 May 1915

Big day papering and painting wee room to the back. Had three rake to the wood for firewood. Society man here. Territorial[s] poaching. Six shots fired in the wood down the Green road. Darling and squad planting gardens. Got my money from London – 10s. This will be my 13 weeks up so my next will only be 5s instead of ten. Mrs Muirhead looking for Henderson, but missed him.

Tuesday 11 May 1915

Letters from Jean, Sandy and Lachie. All well, but Sandy's wee boy, Alick, who is not getting any better.

Tuesday 11 May, continued

Very wet day so I am confined to the house. Bella is finishing the house cleaning and I am amusing myself clearing up and writing nonsense.

Wednesday 12 May 1915

Went to Leith and saw a saw doctor[78] at the Links. Left a bit of a byke at The Cala Company, Leith Walk. Could not get a book case, and came home very tired. Walked all the way to Leith.

Thursday 13 May 1915

Had some bad shots of my head [pains]. Jean and Flo from Edinburgh. Both quite pleased with themselves. I couldn't convoy them home, but Bella went with them so far.

Friday 14 May 1915

Went to Queensferry and saw the doctor and got a certificate and stayed at home all day after.

Saturday 15 May 1915

Went to Dalmaney, Edinburgh and Portobello. Saw Bessie and Uncle Rob. Got 4£ of Society money and came home early.

Sunday 16 May 1915

Bob came on Saturday night from Haddington. He is looking well. Mrs Ramage up from Dalmeny. She's a howler in her new mournings.

Monday 17 May 1915
No letters from anyone.

Tuesday 18 May 1915
Paid Bowmaker.

Tuesday 18 May 1915
Stayed at home. Working cutting sticks.

Wednesday 19 May 1915

Walked to Leith with my cross-cut saw to the [saw] doctor, and came home with the day train. Very tired.

Thursday 20 May 1915

Had a big day trying my new sharpened saw. Got up about half ton of good firewood

Friday [21] May 1915

Went to the Ferry and saw the doctor and called on Davie coming home.

Saturday 22 May 1915

Mrs Stenhouse here from Edinburgh with Mrs Atkinson and Jamie and Bella's boys. Mrs Stenhouse lost her fur necklet, poor soul. Willie here from the camp at Hedderwick. He is looking well.

Sunday 23 May 1915

Willie and Jean both here. Jean and I went to the Dalmaney Station with Willie, and Mrs Ramage came up with us. [...]

Monday 24 May 1915

Went to Barnton. Got my saw – 4d to pay.

Tuesday 25 May 1915

Bella and I went to Barnton to a sale of furniture, which didn't come off so we came up through Craigehall ground.

Wednesday 26 May 1915

Went to Barnton to sale which didn't come on. Letter from Bob. He has listed in the Flying Corps as a carpenter. We got him home at night and he and I went to Queensferry.

Thursday 27 May 1915

Bob away to Edinburgh and Portobello, and to call on Jean en passant. Bella and I carrying sticks and cross-cutting trees. No letters today.

Friday 28 May 1915

Went away with Bob and parted with him on the top of Craigie Hill en route for Dalmaney, on his way to Glencorse to join the Royal Flying Corps as a carpenter. Afterwards staying at home all day, cutting firewood all day.

Saturday 29 May 1915

Went to Dalmaney for my pension money. Called on Doctor Dickson and came home by the Ferry. Jean writes. Bob called on her on his way to Haddington to obtain his trade qualifications. So he may be home again before he goes further afield. Had a great scare with the chimney going on fire, but happily no bad results. Bella took ill owing to the fright we got. Cyclist knocking us up at 2.30.

Sunday 30 May 1915

Went to Cramond Brig [Post Office] for letters and got my National Insurance letter and money. Bella and I took a walk to Queensferry and got a look at the Forth Bridge and Hawe's Pier, and saw where Angus was stationed antebellum. Went up by Dalmeny and had tea with Mrs D Ramage. The boys were up while we were away.

Monday 31 May 1915

Letters from Willie and Lachie. Both going on well. Had a big day carrying sticks and sawing them up. Also Dave and Mrs Muirhead doing [the same].

Tuesday 1 June 1915

Letters from Sandy, Bob and Jamie. They are all well. Also

letter from Linlithgow settling up Angus' affairs – £3 1s 3d
which he had paid into the Police Superanuation Fund. Bob has
not got away yet, but is still at Sunnyside with Coltart. Sandy's
wife and boy are both getting better and Mrs Mc_ is going to
Edinburgh to leave them soon. Jamie may come home tomorrow, but is not sure if he'll get away.

Wednesday 2 June 1915
Busy carrying in firewood. Got a letter from George. They are
all well.

Thursday 3 June 1915
Met Bob and Jamie at Cramond Brig and came home with
them. Bob has no word yet from the Flying Corps.

Friday 4 June 1915
Bob and Jim left for home and I took a run into Edinburgh in
the afternoon. Lachie [here] from Peebles.

Saturday 5 June 1915
Lachie went down to the Ferry with me – to the doctor – so we
had a nice walk. Letter from Bob. He goes to Farnborough on
Monday morning but doesn't know if he will need to go to
Glencorse first.

Sunday 6 June 1915
Lachie here all day and took a walk with Davie's laddies. We
took a walk to Carlowrie.

Monday 7 June 1915
Lachie left at 5.45 and got the first train to Peebles from
Waverly Station.

Tuesday 8 June 1915
Bob left for Farnborough yesterday and sent us a postcard from
London. He had got so far on his journey.

Wednesday 9 June 1915
Knocking about all day, doing little or nothing.

Thursday 10 June 1915
Went to Edinburgh with Bella to the Store, and got measured
for a suit. Willie here. When we got home he was at the dentist's,
getting teeth drawn and stopped. He [has] had a bad week with
his head so he got a good sleep and seemed better.

Friday 11 June 1915
Went down to Craigie Hall with Willie and saw him away
home. He had to call at the dentist's en passant and call on Jean.

Saturday 12 June 1915
Went to the Ferry for Doctor's Certificate. Then to Edinburgh
and got my money and on to Portobello. Uncle Bob and I took
a run to Sevenhall and got home very tired. Banked 35£ with
the Co-op, 24£ was Bob's.

Sunday 13 June 1915
Mrs Ramage and the boys up seeing us. Took a walk round the
hill by Sanders.

Monday 14 June 1915
Letter from Lachie, so I wrote him and Jean.

Tuesday 15 June 1915
Letter from Sandy, Andrew and Bob. They are all well.

Wednesday 16 June 1915
Wrote to George, Andrew and Bob, Jamie and Aunt Nell.

Thursday 17 June 1915
Letter from Aunt Eliza. They are all well and she has had
George seeing her since they flitted.

Friday 18 June 1915

Letter from Bob asking his mother's age as he is making her an allotment from his pay. So she answered it and sent on his razor strop and brush, and I took them down to Cramond Brig. Cut the feet of Mrs Muirhead's drawers to fit the bookcase.

Saturday 19 June 1915

Got a settlement of Angus' back pay from War Office £2 2s 7d and the other half divided among my family 5s 4d to six of them, 5s 3d to two. Lachie and Jean got the small portions.

Sunday 20 June 1915

Jean here from Edinburgh. Wrote to Sandy, Bob and Lach. Took a walk with Bella round Craigie Hill.

Monday 21 June 1915

Went to Edinburgh and drew my money at the GPO, but they would not give me Bob's and Lach's. So I sent on the order to them both to sign, and I could draw it later. Got myself measured for a coat at Curran's, South Brig. Wrote Bob and Lachie on the roadside.

Tuesday 22 June 1915

Had a quiet day. Sawing up firewood and lay about all day.

Wednesday 23 June 1915

Had a big day carrying sticks and went to Dalmaney and brought up bedding-out plants in a hired van − 3s 6d and 7s to Willie − 10s 6d, pretty dear plants.

Thursday 24 June 1915

Wrote to Bob. He is getting on fine. I am to send three photos to Sunnyside.

Friday 25 June 1915

Letters [to Lachie] returned open. Not found in the 2/8, 3/8 or 2/5.[79] Perhaps he's away to make munitions of war.

Saturday 26 June 1915

Went to the Ferry and drew my pension and got the Doctor's Certificate. Got a letter from Sandy.

Sunday 27 June 1915

Lay about all fore-noon. The boys up after dinner. Bella and I took a walk round Craigie Wood.

Monday 28 June 1915

Was twice at Barnton. Got the golf course man to drive Jean home with her trunk.

Tuesday 29 June 1915

Went to Peebles and got Lachie. Asleep in his tent, alright. He got a surprise when I arrove. His letters were never delivered at 3/8 at all.

Wed 30 June 1915

Jamie here at 5.00 a.m. – cycled from Haddington. He mended the roof for me and harried sparrows for me. I and he went to see *Rob Roy* [film].

Thursday 1 July 1915

Jamie left at 7.30 for home. I had another day sawing sticks. Jean at Portobello and Edinburgh shopping and brought home her cycle.

Friday 2 July 1915

No word from Lachie. We are wondering if he is on a recruiting march in East Lothian.

Saturday 3 July 1915

Took a walk to Craigie Brae and saw the home of old Steve Irvine. It's a nice place to look at, but it was hot walking.

Sunday 4 July 1915

Lay about all day and wrote letters to the boys. Mrs Ramage and the boys here in the afternoon.

Monday 5 July 1915

Took a walk to south end of Craigie Wood with Jean, and saw Kirkliston and Carlowrie.

Tuesday 6 July 1915

Got a letter from Bob. He is on for an Officer's Servant [batman] and asking for £2, to keep his pocket and pay accounts. So I went to Cramond Brig and posted it for him. Jean at Edinburgh on her byke. Am to get a cart load of wood from Sounis & Spears for 4/-.

Wed 7 July 1915

Am trying to get Sounis & Spears to drive me up a cart load of wood but can't say till they see Reg Will.

Thursday 8 July 1915

Expecting Willie from Dunbar for four days, but he didn't turn up. Bella waited up till 12.00 a.m. for him.

Friday 9 July 1915

Old man Johnston got his leg broken by falling off a cart load of dung. Coming home from Barnton, his horse ran away and couped the cart in the middle of the road. He was taken to Edinburgh Infirmary.

Saturday 10 July 1915

Willie arrove from Dunbar. Was at Edinburgh – Portobello –

and drew my pension money. Went and saw Short about his letter. He's in a hurry to reduce it by 25s.

Sunday 11 July 1915
Had Flora McLean [niece], Mrs Becint and Jean Waldie visiting. Jean, Mr David and his son, George, here from Dalmeny.

Monday 12 July 1915
Willie and Jean coasting round by Kirkliston to the Ferry.

Tuesday 13 July 1915
Willie left for Dunbar. Jean and I went to Barnton with him. The mater stopped at Cramond Brig and drew Lachie's allowance.

Wednesday 14 July 1915
Jean went to Edinburgh to see sogers' recruiting parade.

Thursday 15 July 1915
Went to Edinburgh and saw James Bertram and was home at dinner time with tea bread for Flora, who enjoyed her visit. Mrs D Ramage met her later.

Friday 16 July 1915
Went down to Dalmaney and had a look round.

Saturday 17 July 1915
Went to Portobello. Bella and I got home on good time. Jean met us at Davie's. Got a prescription from Dr Dickson.

Sunday 18 July 1915
Went to Church with Jean. David and Allan up here in the afternoon. Motor accident at Barnbougle. Two ship's officers hurt.

Monday 19 July 1915

Jean went to Post Office with my London letter. Wrote to Aunt Nell.

Tuesday 20 July 1915

Lying about all day. Got a letter from Dod [son, George, in Canada]. He has bought 160 acres more, making 840.

Wednesday 21 July 1915

Lay about all day doing nought.

Thursday 22 July 1915

Found a lot of crab apples and gathered a few pounds. Miss Brand from Edinburgh, calling on Jean.

Friday 23 July 1915

Picking more crab apples. Jeanie at Edinburgh on her byke.

Saturday 24 July 1915

Went to Dalmaney Station with Jean en route for Dunfermline to visit Betress. Her old mate put her in the train with old Blyth of Tynninghame. Got my pension money and called on the doctor coming home by the Ferry. Went to meet Jean and fell in with Willie who was here to bid us good-bye before going away to the war. He is going [to] Salisbury Plain.

Sunday 25 July 1915

Took a walk down the Almond-side to Craigiehall Bridge, past the Grotto.

Monday 26 July 1915

Lay about all day at home.

Tuesday 27 July 1915

Had a bad turn and never went far.

Wednesday 28 July 1915

Was up before my clothes were on. Down at Carlowie and at Barnbougle for fish. Jamie came here at 5.00 a.m. and wakened us up. He and Jean went to Edinburgh.

Thursday 29 July 1915

Jamie went away home. Willie left Hedderwick for Salisbury Plain. We are all very sad.

Friday 30 July 1915

Postcard from Jamie. Got home all right. Jean at Dalmaney. Very quiet. Took a walk to Dalmaney Home Farm and went by Burnshot *AR*.

Saturday 31 July 1915

Went and got a Doctor's Certificate. Went and came [back] by the Hall. Postcard from Willie from Bamburgh en route for Salisbury Plain. No word of Lachie being at Edinburgh. Got Willie's money from Prestonkirk. Exciseman here seeing Bella. Jean and I took a walk to Barnbougle, to castle, and came up by the Linchold.

Sunday 1 August 1915

No word from anyone. Lachie [has] not turned up at Edinburgh or he would have been here.

Monday 2 August 1915

Bob coming on Saturday to see Lachie.

Tuesday 3 August 1915

Blank.

Wed 4 August 1915

Jean at Edinburgh seeing [nephew] Alick Ramage's wife – very hard up.

Thursday 5 August 1915
Carrying sticks.

Friday 6 August 1915
Old Dickson caught me sawing sticks

Saturday 7 August 1915
Went to Queensferry, Edinburgh and Portobello. Bob and
Lachie both here when I arrove.

Sunday 8 August 1915
Bob at East Linton and Sunnyside, and Haddington seeing Jim.
Stayed at home all day. Lachie very quiet.

Monday 9 August 1915
Bob arrove. He found all well and went off to his regiment by
the last train from Edinburgh. Lachie and Jean saw him to
Barnton.

Tuesday 10 August 1915
Lachie and Jean at Portobello. They have both been very quiet.

Wednesday 11 August 1915
Lachie went off by the first train to Peebles. I went to Stow
[Selkirkshire] to A Ramage's wife's funeral and got a drookin
comin home.

Thursday 12 August 1915
Very hot day and a lot of thunder.

Friday 13 August 1915
More thunder – very alarming here. I stayed at home carrying
sticks.

Saturday 14 August 1915
Went to the Ferry, to the doctor, and lay about all day.

Sunday 15 August 1915
Went to Cramond Brig and got my letter from London, reduced to five bob now. Very quiet day. Jean went to Golf Hall.

Monday 16 August 1915
Carrying up stick all day.

Tuesday 17 August 1915
Letter[s] from Lachie and Jamie. Lachie being made Lance Corporal.

Wed 18 August 1915
Lay about all day. Andrew's birthday again [son, in Canada].

Thursday 19 August 1915
Mr Tennant here calling on me. He is on holiday. Letter from Short asking for news. Been in bed all afternoon. Not so well.

Friday 20 August 1915
Felt very unwell and went to bed early.

Saturday 21 August 1915
Took a trip to Dunfermline. Saw Mrs Barber nee Betress Hart and we had a big day in The Carnegie Park and gardens.[80] Saw Mrs Mason nee Jenny Bull and called on her in the evening. Before we left [we] saw her mother, who stayes with her. Got home at 9.00 p.m. Left Jean to stay all night and come home on Sunday.

Sunday 22 August 1915
Signed and sent away all my SO papers. Have only to send Lloyd George a Cert[ificate] 1 in fourteen days.

Monday 23 August 1915

Got a letter from Lachie. He is Orderly this week, and getting on fine.

Tuesday 24 August 1915

Went to Portobello en family and stayed with Aunt Nell all day. Uncle Rab, Jean and I went out on the Pier.[81] I have not been on it for over thirty years. Great changes since then, but the sea and sands is ever the same.

Wednesday 25 August 1915

Jamie here from Haddington at 5.00 a.m. After he got a sleep, he went with Jean cycling to Queensferry. Letter from […].

Thursday 27 August 1915

Jamie sick all night and away home. Very hard up and going to take the train from Edinburgh.

Friday 28 August 1915

Postcard from Jamie. He got home alright and went on duty, but very hard up. Went to the Ferry, so did Jean.

Sunday 29 August 1915

Bella and I went to the Kirk and saw Davie and his boys and Julian through the window. Jean came home alright.

Monday 30 August 1915

Went to Cameron Toll en route for Dalkieth, but turned and went away home again. Saw John Stark from Dunbar wi his motor. Wet day in Edinburgh.

Tuesday 31 August 1915

Willie arrove from Longbridge on furlough for five days, before he goes to the war. He was very tired with the journey.

Wednesday 1 September 1915

Wet fore-noon. Willie went off to Haddington to see Jamie, and on to East Linton to see his friends there and got home at 11.30 p.m. after I was in my bed. Very tired.

Thursday 2 September 1915

Jean and I went with Willie to Princes Street Station and saw him away to Crewe with the 2.00 p.m. Cally train. He was a bit cut up – first time ever I saw him sad looking.

Friday 3 September 1915

Big day at the wood. Got a Doctor's Certificate from the doctor here.

Saturday 4 September 1915

Went to Edinburgh and Portobello and nearly had a row with Young about the SO. He's a bit snotty, is Young. Uncle Rob no better. Lachie here when I arrove home. He went off by the 8.00 p.m. train from Barnton. Jean went down with him.

Sunday 5 September 1915.

Never left the place all day. Jean Waldie and Mrs D Ramage here in the afternoon. Also the two boys from Dalmeny.

Monday 6 September 1915

Asked [for] a pass and PJ[82] to Manchester Station Master Holidaying.

Tuesday 7 September 1915

Davie here with a paper for me to fill up, applying for a PJ.

Wed 8 September 1915

Lay about all day and cut up firewood in the evening.

Thursday 9 September 1915
Do. Do. [Ditto Ditto].
Mrs McDonald here from Edinburgh.

Friday 15 September 1915
Went to ask about pass, which I got. But no PJs. Saw Dr Dickson and told him I was going away.

Saturday 11 September 1915
Still no word of PJ, so we can't go away as intended.

Sunday 12 September 191
Thirty two years since I lost my arm at Portobello. Took a walk round, but did not go anywhere.

Monday 13 September 1915
Went to Dalmeny Station. Still no word from Edinburgh.

Tuesday 14 September 1915
Got my order for PJ Carlisle to Manchester.

Wednesday 15 September 1915
Left Dalmeny at 8.56 a.m. for Edinburgh. Left Edinburgh at 10.30 a.m. for Carlisle. Left Carlisle at 1.00 p.m. for Manchester, after plenty time for PJs. Sandy met us at Chelford and drove us up in car. Found all well.

Thursday 16, Friday 17, Saturday 18, Sunday 19, Monday 20, Tuesday 21, Wednesday 22, Thursday 23 – left for home.

Friday 24 September 1915
Rested all day. Very tired.

Saturday 25 September 1915
Great fightin on Western Front. Great slaughter, great victory

for the British. Lot of Scotsmen killed [from] the highland regiments.

Intervening space left out – nothing to record.

Saturday 9 October 1915

Jamie brought home his trunk, so that's the end of an old story. He has joined the MMP.[83] and is getting a few days to bid goodbye.

Sunday 10 October 1915

Took a bit walk [with] family. Passed a very quiet day.

Monday 11 October 1915

Jim and Jean at Portobello. Lachie at Edinburgh Castle. Sent a telegram for fear Jim went to Peebles and he [might be] away.

Tuesday 12 October 1915

Wet day. Lay about all day. Jim lost his trip to Peebles.

Wed 13 October 1915

Jamie, Jean and I went in to Edinburgh to see Lachie. We called on Mrs McDonald and then went [South]park, Cannongate, Holyrood Road and went up to the Castle esplanade and waited till he got off duty. Jean and I came home by the 5.40 p.m. train and Jim went to the theatre with Lach and came home later.

Thursday 14 October 1915

Jamie and I took a trip to Kirkcaldy, The Lang Toon, and had a fine journey there and back, but it was very foggie and we couldn't get a very good view of Edinburgh as we thought we would. Awfully busy toon, making floorcloth and cork lino.[84]

Friday 15 October 1915

Jamie left Dalmeny for Glencorse at 8.56 a.m. I went and saw him away and thense to the doctor and got a certificate and my pension money and came home by the Halls.

Saturday 16 October 1915

Postcard from Jamie. He left Edinburgh for Aldershott last night. Lachie was at theatre with him. Lachie arrove here from the Castle in the afternoon. I went down in the morning and saw John Devlin for some herrings.

Sunday 17 October 1915

Lachie and I took a walk round Craigie Wood and lay about all day. Maggie Brand here from Edinburgh and they went away together for the 9.00 p.m. train. I wrote to Bob, Willie and Sandy.

Monday 18 October 1915

Very wet day. Never was out all day.

Tuesday 19 October 1915

Letter from Bob and Jamie – both well.

Wednesday 20, Thursday 21 October 1915

Wet days – nothing doing.

Friday 22 October 1915

Bella, Jean and I at Edinburgh. Did not see Lachie. Lost the train and came home in bus.

Saturday 23 October 1915

Took down a [turbit] to Davie at Dalmaney and he and I went down to the station. No word of Jamie's parcel. Got a wetting coming home.

Sunday 24 October 1915

Jean at the Kirk. Lachie and Flora McLean came after dinner, and left for the 9.00 p.m.

Monday 25 October 1915

Very cold day and don't feel well. J Kilpatrick has listed – and both the Jonsons – into the R[oyal] Han[overians]. Old Henderson is in a funk and trying to get them back. Got a cart of coal.

Tuesday 26 October 1915

One year has passed away since Angus was killed near Ypres and was buried in a trench where he fell. So much has been crowded into my life since that, I have never been the same. Broken in body and spirit I had to leave our old home and go forth to wander the earth, lonely and sad. Still I have plenty to thank God for, and be thankfull for having so many left. And plenty have lost their only, and some their all, in this awful war carried on with cruelty indescribable and all in the name of God – the God of love and mercy.

Wednesday 27 October 1915

Got Jamie's allotment paper [...]. Walked to Corstorphine and back via the Drum Brae.

Thursday 28 October 1915

Went to Cramond Brig looking for carrots, but didn't get any.

Friday 29 October 1915

Went to the doctor and got a certificate for National Insurance. Also to the station and got my pension. Then down the steps to the Halls and couldn't got any carrots. Spoke to Mr McLaren's clerk about a house for a home.

Saturday 30 October 1915

Went with Bella to Portobello. Got my SO money from Mr

Young. Uncle Rab very hard up. Got my [National] Insurance money at Cramond Brig and got home at 6.30 p.m. Jean at Edinburgh.

Sunday 31 October 1915

Jean away to the Kirk. Lachie arrove from Linton. He stayed with T Denholm all Saturday night. Cassidy away to North Berwick.

Monday 1 November 1915

Carried and cut sticks. Lachie went away to the Castle.

Tuesday 2 November 1915

Went down to Dalmeny with a parcel for Davie. Jean in Edinburgh [overnight].

Wednesday 3 November 1915

Sent away parcels to W H [son] and W A [nephew] Ramage and carried sticks all day.

Thursday 4 November 1915

No letters. Carried sticks and cut them up. Very quiet [today].

Friday 5 November 1915

Jean at Edinburgh. Went to Queensferry. Met Davie at Barnbougle Gate and he walked with me to Halls Brae. Old Miss Glendinning with the paper. She's an old cadger.

Saturday 6 November 1915

Took a long walk to Granton, round by Barnton Dykes. Lost myself and went through a private estate and came out at a gate with two eagles.[85] Down by the Edinburgh Gas work to Granton Pier. Thense to Golden Acre and home by Inverleith Road and Davidson's Mains. Lachie came from the Castle, looking well.

Sunday 7 November 1915

Jean at the Kirk and we all went down in the afternoon to Davie's to meet Aunt Eliza [wife of brother, James] from Berwickshire.

Monday 8 November 1915

Went down and saw Davie and bargained with him to take a quarter sheep at […]lb. Jean took it down at night and Dav[ie] came up with her. No word from any of the boys.

Tuesday 9 November 1915

Still no word from the boys, but Jim, I forgot Jim, poor chap.

Wed 10 November 1915

Got a demand for 6£ for rent. Went down and saw Aunt Eliza but she was affraid to come to Craigie for the cold. So [t]he journey is off. Wrote to Bob. Jean away down.

Thursday 11 November 1915

Jamie arrove from Aldershot. Been lying all night at Edinburgh Waverly Station. Very cold.

Friday 12 November 1915

Jamie went to Haddington and bade good-bye to his mates. He has a very bad cold.

Saturday 13 November 1915

Went to Edinburgh with Jim, and saw him and Carr away in the 14 army NE for London and Aldershot. Went and saw Melville and Lindsay about my house and gave it up for the 28th December.

Sunday 14 November 1915

Very quiet day. Stayed at home all day.

Monday 15 November 1915

Went to Dalkeith house hunting. Walked by Lasswade and Loanhead to Straiton and took the Bus to Edinburgh.

Tuesday 16 November 1915

Got a letter from Bob and Jean. Bella and I walked to Kirkliston and bargained for a house there.

Wed 17 November 1915

Got a postcard from Willie. He's off to Serbia, poor chap, via the Mediterannean. [He] says not to expect a letter for a week or two.

Thursday 18 November 1915

Sawed sticks all day.

Friday 19 November 1915

Jean at Edinburgh. No letters, only circular from Lady Clemantine Warring.[86] Guager here at Bella.

Saturday 20 November 1915

No more allowance for Bella. Went and gave up house at Kirkliston. Got a letter from M J McLean [niece] saying her brother died yesterday. Called on D Ramage. He is going to the funeral on Monday at Selkirk. Poor chap, he [McLean] did not last long after he went home from Milton.

Sunday 21 November 1915

Lachie here from Edinburgh. Stayed at home all day.

Monday 22 November 1915

Davie was at Erick McLean's funeral at Selkirk. It was too cold for me.

Tuesday 23 November 1915
Bella, Jean and I were in Edinburgh, house-hunting, but did not come on.

Wed 24 November 1915
Went down to see Davie and he said he was going to see his brother, Alick, at Bellahouston Hospital, Glasgow, so I promised to go.

Thursday 25 November 1915
Went to Glasgow and saw Erick Ramage. He is getting better, and was pleased to see us both.

Friday 26 November 1915
Lay about all day and cut some sticks, etc.

Saturday 27 November 1915
Went to Dalmeny, Edinburgh and Portobello and saw Aunt Nell and did my business. Got a letter from Inverkeithing about a hen farm, but I don't think I'll take it. It's too far from a station and will be too big for me to tackle myself.

Sunday 28 November 1915
Lachie came last night, and Maggie Brand today. So they went off together for the nine train. Wrote to Dykes and refused the hen farm. Also to Sandy and Bob. Have not got my Lloyd George[87] this week yet.

Monday 29 November 1915
Jean away to Edinburgh GPO to try for a sorter's place. I went and saw the doctor and got a certificate and paid my Parish Council Rates and lay about all day. Postcard from Willie from somewhere in the south of France. Very glad to hear from him.

Tuesday 30 November 1915

Letter for Jean, but she's away. Mrs Muirhead off to Roslin to see her daughter. Cut sticks all forenoon and was going to Gogar but took the rue and stayed at home.

Wednesday 1 December 1915

Went to Murrayfield by train and walked to Stenhousemill and back by Gorgie Road and Tynecastle to Edinburgh. Called on Mr Lindsay and made a bargain for over the New Year at least. Very tired when I got home. No news of Jim yet, poor chap.

Thursday and Friday, 2 and 3 December

Busy cutting and carrying stick. Got letters from Willie and Bob. Both well.

Saturday 4 December 1915

Went to Davidson's Mains and saw Store Manager about balance, and got a bob taken. The rest was all right.

Sunday 5 December 1915

Lachie came here last night and is having a days rest. He has passed his exam and passed for a shoeing smith so he won't be long at the Castle now. He went off for the 9.00 p.m. Cala [Caledonian] Passenger.

Monday 6 December 1915

Very stormy day. Jean going to Portobello to stay with Aunt Nell all night and get some things for her cousin, Billie, for Christmas.

Tuesday 7 December 1915

Went to Cramond Brig with Bella for her allowances at the Post Office. Met Mrs Imrie, but didn't know her at first. Got a postcard from Jamie.

Wednesday 8 December 1915

Had a big day carying and cutting wood, and prepairing for a storm of snow. Was very hard up after I got through. Bella got her leg hurt with a flying splinter.

Thursday 9 December 1915

Snow storm. Letter from Bob. He is shifted to another Fort at Gosport. He says they have turned him into a housemaid. Old Willie Walker died at East Linton and Dadie McLean at Tynninghame.

Friday 10 December 1915

Postcard from old Haidly Smith saying he had let the Haits Smithy. Lay about all day. No letters, but a postcard from Willie to Bella and Jean. So I wrote to PB.

Saturday 11 December 1915

Letter from Willie. He is well and enjoying himself, so I answered him and Sandy. Doctor here and signed my Certificate.

Sunday 12 December 1915

Sent away letters to Sandy, Willie and Bob. Wrote to Dod and Andrew. Went to South Queensferry and posted the first and kept the other two over. Called on Davie, who walked round with me to Chapel Gate [Dalmeny Estate]. Met old and young Sanders on Dolphinton Brae.

Monday 13 December 1915

Lachie here from Peebles Direct and went home to the Castle to be ready for the road to Falkirk on Tuesday morning. He called on Maggie Brand and got a pair of socks and a towel.

Tuesday 14 December 1915

Down at Barnton Station ordering coal, and Bella was at the Post Office for her money.

Wednesday 15 December 1915

No sign of coal. Very wet day, so there was some […].

Thursday 16 December 1915

Went down to Dalmeny and got some cement for mending the house – and having a big job carying it up.

Friday 17 December 1915

Built up the lobby […] and cut wood for firing.

Saturday 18 December 1915

Cut and trailed sticks all day. Hurt and tore my left ear with a big tree top [while] coming down the hill from the rocks. Got a letter from Bob. He is well. Wrote to him and Lach at night. Jean left for Edinburgh to stay all night.

Sunday 19 December 1915

Went down to the Post Office and posted letters to Bob and Lach. No letters. Lay about all day. It was so cold. Alick Ramage up from Dalmeny. His mother awa to Aldairn and Davie's keeping house.

Monday 20 December 1915

Lay about all day and broke sticks.

Tuesday 21 December 1915

Went down to Barnton with Sandy's bag and his Christmas loaf. Ordered coal a second time.

Wednesday 22 December 1915

Very wet day. Got up coal – 10 cwt.

Thursday 23 December 1915

Went down with Mrs Johnston to Cramond Brig to post a […] to Aunt Eliza

Friday 24 December 1915

Went to the Ferry and got my Certificate and called on Davie. Mrs Ramage got on grand at Aldairn.

Saturday 25 December 1915

Christmas day. Bella and I went to Portobello and got our Christmas dinner with Aunt Nell. Letter from Jim, from Egypt.

Sunday 26 December 1915

Mrs Ramage up, and got her tea with us. Jean here – she is going back for another week at the General Post Office.

Monday 27 December 1915

Jean left here for her work in an awfull storm.

Tuesday 28 December 1915

Went with Bella to Post Office and went to Barnton for my coat [which] Jean took away with her. Bob arove at 2.00 a.m. from Edinburgh – walked all the road.

Wed 29 December 1915

Letter from Lachie telling us what a happy Christmas he had, and thanking us for his parcel. Bob having bad wet weather at East Linton.

Thursday 30 December 1915

Erick and Davie Ramage, and his two boys, here. Sandy sent a telegram saying he was sending on a bot[tle] for the New Year. Got receipt for Kate's from Lithgow and a letter from Mrs Stenhouse.

Friday 31 December 1915

Went to Portobello with Bob and Jean, and I saw him away by the Caledonian Railway, Princes Street to Chelford all right.

Saturday 1 January 1916

Another year has come and gone, and other three of my sons have listed – two serving and one attested under Lord Derby's Scheme, Group 41.[88] So that's five. Had old Fitzpatrick for my first foot, also D M Head. That was all the strangers in my house this year, so everything passed off quietly, and we were all quite happy.

Sunday 2 January 1916

Flory McLean here visiting us from Edinburgh. Jean and I went down the road with, and saw her safely away. She had a bad cold.

Monday 3 January 1916

Went to Edinburgh and bought a few things to send to Willie and Jamie. Big crowd going to the Powderhall races and sports.[89] You would think there was no war going on.

Tuesday 4 January 1916

Wet morning, but cleared up at dinnertime and Bella and I walked down to Cramond Brig Post Office for her allowances.

Wednesday 5 January 1916

Carrying and cutting sticks all day. Jean went to [Golf Hall] and walked home in the dark.

Thursday 6 January 1916

Cut and carried sticks till dinner. D Ramage got some with us, and I got him to cut my hair. Too wet to work all afternoon so I just took a walk over the hill.

Friday 7 January 1916

Stayed at home and cut sticks. Jean in Edinburgh. Bella and I met her.

Saturday 8 January 1916

Went down and saw the doctor and stayed at home all day after. Miss Waldie came to stay till tomorrow.

Sunday 9 January 1916

Miss Waldie and Jean Walker over to the church to Dalmeny. Wet afternoon.

Monday 10 January 1916

Trench card from Willie from Salonika and a letter from Sandy. They are all well. Went to Seaton Mill, but the house was let. So I walked round by Blinkbonny Meadow Mill and Preston-pans where I took the electric car to Joppa and the cable to Edinburgh.[90] When I got near home I met George Ramage [nephew], who called en route for Dalmeny. He was just out of the Edinburgh Infirmary.

Tuesday 11 January 1916
Carried and cut wood all day.

Wednesday 12 January 1916

Do. Do. [Ditto Ditto] Jean away to Portobello. Went to Barnton for Muirhead's *Scotsman* with Mr Johnston. Came up by Craigiehall. Mrs Muirhead got a soldier for a lodger for a month. He is going to work on the farm with Henderson.

Thursday 13 January 1916

Cutting and carrying sticks. Went down to Burnfoot to meet Jean coming from Edinburgh. She was in putting her name in [the] register.[91]

Friday 14 January 1916

Big day cutting wood and Bella and I carried it home. Lady in motor seeking Jean for a table maid.

Saturday 15 January 1916

Jean went and hired herself to go to a Doctor Sinclair in Edinburgh. He's an eye specialist. Got a notice to send in my bank book to Mr Laing. Also a long letter from Mr Tennant, East Linton.

Sunday 16 January 1916

Mrs Ramage and Allan here. No word from the boys across. Stayed at home all day.

Monday 17 January 1916

Went to Edinburgh and gave in my bank book to Laing, to be made up for year. Went up the High Street, to Mound, and bought some stationary. Came home very tired. Got a rabbit as a present from the young keeper.

Tuesday 18 January 1916

No letters from the boys. We are wearying to hear from them. The War Office won't give us an allowance for Jamie. […] We are not disappointed, as we never expected it. James Darling no better, according to Fitzpatrick.

Wednesday 19 January 1916

Went to Cramond Brig Post Office for a *Scotsman* newspaper and two picture papers. Got a letter from Lachie. He is very busy just now, but well and cheery. He was at Bo'ness with J Grant of Dunbar and had a good day. No word from any of the other boys. Took a walk down by the railway and saw all the navies working at the slip on the bank. Very cold wet day for them. No news from Salonika, only rumours. Never seen Mr Johnson today, owing to the wet day.

[…]

Thursday 20 January 1916

Mrs Johnston down telling us about Henderson proposing to

reduce their money by half. But I could not advise her. Very wet stormy day. Never went anywhere. Two letters from Willie – they were posted on different dates but both arrove at once here. He is well, and writes quite cheerily.

Friday 21 January 1916
Carried some sticks, and half-soled my boots. Too stormy for anything. Wrote to Willie at night.

Saturday 22 January 1916
Went to Portobello and Edinburgh. Was at a Burns concert in George Street Hall [and] got tea with Flora, who was with us.

Sunday 23 January 1916
Took a long walk by the Drum Brae, Corstorphine Bank, East Craigs and home by Craigiehall. Very tired. Maggie Brand here. Jean saw her to Barnton Station and Bella and I met her opposite Low Wood. Very stormy night. Sent away a letter to Lachie.

Monday 24 January 1916
Went down and saw Doctor Dickson and got some messages from the Ferry. Called on D Ramage en passing. Got my pension at the station. No letters today. Got my old pass taken from me, and went and got a new one from the police.

Tuesday 25 January 1916
Took a walk round the hill and went down to Cramond Bridge with Bella. Very windy stormey day. Jean at Edinburgh and home at 5.00 p.m. Got letters from Bob and Sandy – both well. Rabbie Burns day.

Wednesday 26 January 1916
Had a big day among the sticks, till the rain came on. Got a letter from Willie, from Salonika. No signs of a fight, he says, so far. Thinks the Bulgars are backing out, and the Germans are

needed elsewhere. Jean busy getting her kist ready for removal tomorrow – if it's God's will to spare her till then.

Thursday 27 January 1916

Jean left for South Charlotte Square for service again. I went down and got Bailey of Cramond to come up for her trunk, and her mother and I went down the road and saw her away. She was very dull all day before she left. Her heart is not in it.

Friday 28 January 1916

Letter from Willie. He is well and cheery, So that's all we can look for under God's providence. No word from poor Jamie yet, so we are wearying to hear from him again.

Saturday 29 January 1916

Letter from Lachie, to his mother. He is going to see Sandy for Wednesday and is needing cash for the journey. Took a walk to Gogar Stane to look at a house, but it's a derelict dairy and no use for us. Came home by Turnhouse and Craigiehall grounds, and was very tired.

Sunday 30 January 1916

Went to Cramond Brig Post Office. Got a letter from cousin, Billy. He is at military school in France. Went to the Ferry and posted a letter to Lach. D Ramage and wife, and our Jean, here when I came back at 5.00 p.m.

Monday 31 January 1916

Another letter from Willy. He is well. No word from Jim so I wrote to him today. Big aerial raid on Paris on Saturday afternoon – twenty four killed. Big day stick-getting on Carlowrie Hill. Bella washing. All quiet here.

Tuesday 1 February 1916

Letter from Jim, from the old spot. He is still at Alexandra and getting on First Class. He didn't go to Mudros after the troops were withdrawn from Dardanelles so we are very pleased he did not go there, as intended.

Wednesday 2 February 1916

Lachie away to Sandy's at Capesthorn. He called on Maggie Brand, en passant.

Thursday 3 February 1916

Went to Dalmany and got a PJ for Edinburgh and put away 12£ in the bank. That['s] 155£ now, mounting up.

Friday 4 February 1916

Bella and I trained from Barnton to Edinburgh where I left her and went off to the Fair at Haddington, where I saw a lot of old friends – George Forsyth and Dickie Jamson, Alick and Stephen Ramage – but not Andrew [Alick, Stephen and Andrew are nephews].

4 February continued

Called at Portobello and got Bella home with me.

Saturday 5 February 1916

Went and saw the doctor who thinks I could be a watchman, but I don't know where I could get a job as one. He is very anxious to get me off his hands.

Sunday 6 February 1916

Lay about all day at home. No word of Lachie. Very stormy weather – great wind. No-one calling.

Monday 7 February 1916

Lachie arrove from Sandy's in the midst of a storm of snow and went away in another. So he's got rough weather, but is looking well.

Tuesday 8 February 1916

No letters. Sent away Sandy's boots per post and lay about all day at home.

Wed 9 February 1916

Still no letters. Jean and Jean Waldie came in the afternoon. Jean is very hard up looking, but quite cheery. Still cold weather and signs of more storms.

Thursday 10 February 1916

Very stormy day. Lay about all day.

Friday 11 February 1916

Letter from Bob. He is alright. No word from Jim.

Saturday 12 February 1916

Went to the Ferry and got papers and baccy and came up by Davie's, but Mrs Ramage was out. But I got him at Chapel Gate with Imrie, Cramond Brig.

Sunday 13 February 1916

Jean and Meg Brand out in the afternoon for a trip. Lay about all day and took one short walk to Barnbougle.

Monday 14 February 1916

Bella washing. Took a walk with old Mr Johnston. Got a letter from Willie. Went [to] Edinburgh.

Tuesday 15 February 1916

My sixty second birthday. Got a quiet day and cut some sticks. Wrote to Aunt Nell.

Wednesday 16 February 1916

Letter from Cousin Billy. He has passed his examination for BSM [Battalion Sargeant Major]. Got two letters – one [was]

from Aunt Nell, wishing me 'Many Happy Returns'. Sent away
a letter and parcel to Willie.

Thursday 17 February 1916
Busy all day, cutting and storing wood. Wrote to Lachie, but my
hand was very shaky.

Friday 18 February 1916
Got a letter from Lachie – and a parcel of clothes – saying he
was shifting from Falkirk – [so] not to write till we heard from
him again.

Saturday 19 February 1916
Lachie [sent] suit and the parcel with postcard enclosed saying
they were off to England, but didn't know where. Went to
Portobello, Bella and I.

Sunday 20 February 1916
Very quiet day here. Didn't go far from home.

Monday 21 February 1916
Lachie has left Falkirk. Got letter from Sandy, with card.

Tuesday 22 February 1916
Letters from Lachie and Jim. Lachie at Chelmsford.

Wednesday 22 February 1916
Wrote to Jim and Lachie, and Lachie was glad to see that Jim
was well.

Thursday 23 February 1916
Sent away a letter to W A Ramage [Billie], to France.

Friday 24 February 1916

Sent a parcel to Bob and went down and registered at Cramond Bridge. Great Battle at Verdun.[92]

Saturday 25 February 1916

Stayed at home all day. Very wet day.

Saturday 26 February 1916 –

Sunday 27 February 1916

Jean here by buss. I went to Barnton to meet her but she was home when I arrove. She was escorted down by Maggie Muirhead['s] young man.

Monday 28 February 1916

Stayed at home all day. Got two letters from Salonika, from Willie. He is well and no word of any sign of the enemy attacking them yet.

Tuesday 29 February 1916

Bella washing. Wrote to Willie and got a letter from Lachie. He is getting on fine at Chelmsford and has got a new mate, a nice, cheery bloke.

Wednesday 1 March 1916

March came in wet and rough. Old Henderson thrashing, [but it] was a very wet day, so they were stuck.

Thursday 2 March 1916

No letters today. So I took a walk down and saw the thrashing mill working and after noon was busy carrying and cutting sticks. Saw a young naval officer and his lady on the hill at three forty-five. Saw a lot of signalling on the Forth, far down beyond Inchkeith. Another air raid on south-east coast of England. One baby killed – nine months old.

Friday 3 March 1916

Letter from Bob. He is well and got his parcel all right. Busy making fire wood all afternoon. Went to the doctor at the Ferry and got bacca and papers. Called on Davie and Mrs Ramage, en passant. Davie came up to Dolphinton with me and had a long crack.

Saturday 4 March 1916

Man on motorbike, no SM555. Kens Imrie, he says. I telt him I'd report him for taking photos. Was at the Ferry for paper. Maggie Muirhead had out Jean's byke at Barnton at 5.00 p.m.

Sunday 5 March 1916

Never went further than the foot of the hill. Very cold. Had two of Davie's boys from Dalmeny. Wrote to Bob and Lachie.

Monday 6 March 1916

Got my London money – twopence charged, letter not stamped. Letters from Sandy and Aunt Nell – all well. Andrew [grandson] has got into the choir to sing. Bella and I busy at the firewood making. Cut my […]. Snowing tonight.

Monday 6 March 1916

Letter from Sandy and Aunt Nell. They are all well. Andrew has got into the choir to sing. Bella and I had a big day at the wood.

Tuesday 7 March 1916

My sister, Agness, died suddenly at Comrie [Perthshire]. Telegram from Colina [niece]. Letter from Jamie from Alexandria. He is well and has got his parcel at last. They've not been in a hurry, but better late than never.

Wednesday 8 March 1916

Lay about all day, and Bella and I cut some sticks. Sent away a letter to Comrie, to Miss Colina McLaren.

Thursday 9 March 1916

Another quiet day. Cut some firewood and lay about at home all day. James Darling popping about. Aggie got a new dress.

Friday 10 March 1916

My sister, Aggie, to be buried today at Comrie. Letter sent from Miss Richie to Willie. Sent back to me by censor. Wonder what's wrong, as it seemed rightly addressed. Hope he's well, poor soul.

Saturday 11 March 1916

Went to the Ferry for bacca. Letter from Jamie. Bill has been calling on him – coming home for a month, he says.

Sunday 12 March 1916

Jeanie and Maggie Brand came out to Barnbougle Lodge with the buss.

Monday 13 March 1916

No letters today, so we had a day at the wood. Been anxious about Willie all day, but he never put in an appearance.

Tuesday 14 March 1916

Very wet day. Letter from Mrs Stenhouse. Jim is in the trenches in France.

Wednesday 15 March 1916

Went to Edinburgh for some goods and garden seeds, from H Harrall. No onion sets to be got. Bella went down to the Post Office with me in the forenoon. Lot of letters from Salonika for Willie.

Thursday 16 March 1916

Very wet cold day. Stayed in the house all day.

Friday 17 March 1916
Cut sticks all day. No word of Willie yet.

Saturday 18 March 1916
Went down to the doctor and lost the first train and [so] went by the 10.50 a.m. Got my money – pension and Guards' Society. Bella got a letter from Willie, after I left, so came on after me with it. Also one from Sandy about his old lady's death and funeral. They are all well. We went down to Portobello and found Uncle Bob and Aunt Nell in their usual [spirits]. Got home all right and called on Davie. They are all well. Mrs D and Allan at Edinburgh. Home at six thirty. Very tired. Letter from Aunt Eliza.

Sunday 19 March 1916
Lay at home all day. Davie's boys up with paper, *The Post*.

Monday 20 March 1916
Letter and parcel from Bob. He is off to France at last, poor chap.

Tuesday 21 March 1916
Another letter from Bob. Bella at Cramond Brig. I went and met her. Wrote to Lachie.

Wednesday 22 March 1916
No letters. Carried sticks all day. Very hard up with my hip joint – overdid the sticks work, I think.

Thursday 23 March 1916
Wrote a letter to Willie, as he may never be away from Alexandria for a long time and be wearying for news.

Friday 24 March 1916
Got a letter from Lachie. He is well and on the cadge from his

mother, So I sent him a ten shilling [note] and went down and
registered the letter at Cramond Bridge Post Office. Got a
few lines from Jean, and a letter for Willie re-adressed from
Salonika.

Saturday 25 March 1916

Went to Edinburgh and did some purchases for my garden.
Awfull storm of snow to come home in. About four inches of
snow on the road before I got home.

Sunday 26 March 1916

Big wreath of snow at top of road – five feet deep. Cameron
ha[d] to break the top off it before he got his old yeoper [horse]
through with the milk cart. Jeanie here from Edinburgh. [I] went
down to the wood with her when she went away.

Monday 27 March 1916

Went to Corstorphine to see about a house, but it's no good.
He's [in] terms with some-one at Loanhead. Letter[s] from
Sandy and Lachie. Both well. Also letter from cousin Billie,
saying he was wounded in right arm and in hospital to undergo
operations.

Tuesday 28 March 1916

Letter from Jim saying Willie was still at Alexandria. Wrote to
him and sent away Willie's letter and a letter to Bill enclosed.
Also wrote to cousin Billie, poor chap, and Sandy and Lachie.

Wednesday 29 March 1916

Busy day at the sticks – on the hill and cutting them up after.

Thursday 30 March 1916

Went to the Dean for a [...] cabbages and was very tired before
I got home – but after a rest, started the wood.

Friday 30 March 1916

Got a letter from Willie. He thinks he may follow it soon, God willing. Men cleaning the cesspool at top of the road, but the drain is choked it seems. Got up a good few sticks from the top of the quarry. Old Moorhead [out], plantin his shallots.

Saturday 1 April 1916

Was at the doctor. No morning papers. Called on Davie and got my hair cut, and went back in afternoon – for fish and with some shallots.

Sunday 2 April 1916

Took a walk down to East Craigie Farm. No sign of Willie yet. Zeppelin raid on Edinburgh. Fire at Leith. Some damage on the Castle Terrace.[93]

Monday 3 April 1916

Willie here from Salonika. He looks very fresh. Letters from Lachie and Aunt Nell. All went to the Ferry and came home by Craig Brae but got my walk for nought. KOSB [King's Own Scottish Borderers] left the Ferry for Edinburgh. No particulars of air raid on Edinburgh and Leith. Saw the fire at Leith blazing at 3.00 a.m.

Tuesday 4 April 1916

Willie in Edinburgh seeing Jean, wrote to Jim saying he [Willie] was here all right.

Wednesday 5 April 1916

Bob's birthday. Sent away a small parcel for him.

Thursday 6 April 1916

Lay about all day. Willie at Dalmany seeing Davie. Got account rendered for rent – £3.

Friday 7 April 1916

Went to pay rent at 110 George Street, but they want five pounds instead of three. Willie and I went on to Portobello and saw Aunt Nell and both her men folks. Adam was as large as life.

Saturday 8 April 1916

Lay about all day. Willie was at Edinburgh afternoon and night. It was very cold. Letter from James.

Sunday 9 April 1916

Never went anywhere. Jean and Jean Waldie here all afternoon. We took a walk round the hill – fine view but cold.

Monday 10 April 1916

Went to Edinburgh and paid my rent to Melvile & Lindsay at 110 George Street so I'm clear up to Whitsunday. Came home early and had a walk up the hill. Letter from Jim on Saturday. Cut some firewood.

Tuesday 11 April 1916

Letter from Sandy. He is getting a job on the motors – a staff job – and is to get a few days before he goes. Willie waiting on for news from Hamilton. He's away to Edinburgh again. Had a long call from Davie.

Wednesday 12 April 1916

Willie at Edinburgh for new clothes and got a new rig out – so he's away to Sandy by the last train.

Thursday 13 April 1916

Letter from Lachie so I wrote him at once (and sent five shillings) so that he would know Willie wasn't here as he might [otherwise] come running away to see him.

Friday 14 April 1916

Big day at the sticks. Jean came when I was busy. She has been ill all week with the influenza.

Saturday 15 April 1916

Went to Edinburgh and got no money. Young said I was over-paid last week fifteen shillings and got me to sign two slips, for fifteen shillings, and tore up the one for thirty shillings [for] last month. Was down seeing Aunt Nell. They are all in their ordinary way.

Sunday 16 April 1916

Lay about all day. Jean went away home. Mrs Ramage did not come up (too wet).

Monday 17 April 1916

Lachie at Capesthorn. Sandy away passing his test – so there was no fun.

Tuesday 18 April 1916

Willie came home from Sandy's and left them all well, and Sandy not home yet.

Wednesday 19 April 1916

Letter from [the] general secretary of the Guards' Society.[94] No more money for me to [be] got out of him. Very wet cold days. Willie at Edinburgh.

Thursday 20 April 1916

Another wet day. Lay about all day.

Friday 21st April 1916

No word from cousin Billy, or any of our boys.

Saturday 22 April 1916

Willie at Edinburgh.

Sunday 23 April 1916

Jean, Flora and Meg Brand from Edinburgh. Flora looking much better and says her father and Mary Jane are both getting on much better. Willie went down with them and Flo lost her fur.

Monday 24 April 1916

Tree top blown down behind old Mary's house so we had a big day cleaning her up – Mrs and Muirhead and us – and I was very tired.

Tuesday 25 April 1916

Went down to Dalmeny and got a PT [post train] to Linton – Willie, Davie and I. We met Mr Clydesdale at the Hall's Battery. They are erecting more batteries and electric flash light in [the] football field.

Wednesday 26 April 1916

We went to East Linton by the CR [Caledonian Railway] from Barnton. Saw a lot of my old friends and got home at 10.30 p.m. Quite fresh. Everything looks well out yonder. Great works going on at East Fortune.[95]

Thursday 27 April 1916

Very tired after my journey. Did some firewood chopping.

Friday 28 April 1916

Another day chopping wood. Willie at Edinburgh in the evening.

Saturday 29 April 1916

Went to the station and doctor. Willie at Edinburgh again. Not so well today.

Sunday 30 April 1916

Mrs Ramage up with a friend at tea. Willie went and saw them home.

Monday 1 May 1916

Willie at Edinburgh. [He] called on Jean and bought a wristlet watch.

Tuesday 2 May 1916

Air raid on north-east of Scotland. No damage done. Some of the Zeps damaged wrecks near [the] Norwegian coast. Willie making preparation to go off to Aldershot.

Wednesday 3 May 1916

Went to Edinburgh with Willie and saw him off to Aldershot by the 10.00 a.m. North Eastern. Got home very tired and sad.

Thursday 4 May 1916

Letters for Willie from Jim. Jim is out ten miles in the desert, mounted again. He is quite well. Jean here from Edinburgh. She got a fright from the Zeps, which never came.

Friday 5 May 1916

Letter from Lachie. He is well and getting scared by the Zeps, and standing too all night.

Saturday 6 May 1916

Postcard from Bill. He got [to] London all safe and was looking about before going on. Very wet day. Young Alick Ramage up from Dalmeny with fish.

Sunday 7 May 1916

Jean and Meg Brand here from Edinburgh. Never left the house all day for [the] rain. Big fight at Verdun. Germans making another bid for victory.

Monday 8 May 1916

Sent away letter for Willie, and cousin Billy and Bob, and took them down to the post afternoon.

Tuesday 9 May 1916

Bella at Cramond Brig. No word of Bob's money yet.

Wednesday 10 May 1916

Cutting sticks.

Thursday 11 May 1916

Had a call off Davie and Imrie. Alick up to sort rhone pipe. Very wet.

Friday 12 May 1916

Went to Portobello and saw Aunt Nell. She's very hard up. Bella and I called on Jean and left her to draw the dividend. We got a very wet night to come home. Bella very hard up.

Saturday 13 May 1916

Went to Dr Dixon and got my certificate. Called on Davie. No word from anyone.

Sunday 14 May 1916

Very quiet day at home. Bella some better.

Monday 15 May 1916

Went to Edinburgh and paid my rent – five pounds. Walked in and came home to Dalmeny Station. Very tired.

Monday 5 June 1916

Letter from Willie. He left Aldershot on June second for Alexandria, for Salonika. Telegram from Kings Cross. Billie Ramage coming today by the North Eastern Railway. Went to Waverly

Station. Met Willie Ramage at 11.00 p.m. with Jean and brought him home in a taxie to old Craigie. He looks well and is quite cheery.

Tuesday 6 June 1916

Took a walk down to Dalmeny house with cousin, Billy, and came home by the Chapel Gate by Dugeon's House and Dolphinton Farm.

Wednesday 7 June 1916

Took a walk down and introduced cousin, Billie, to his cousin, David. Thence down to the Ferry and had a walk over the Forth Bridge along with Davie and Mr Hunter, the Chief Engineer, and had a grand view. Davie was up at night wi[th] cousin Billie and I went by train to Bonnyrigg, Cockpen and Dalhousie and Butlerfield and showed him Redheugh [Farm] where his father was born. Called on Jean and arranged to meet her tomorrow. Got the train to Barnton and got a wet night to come home.

Thursday 8 June 1916

Left here for Edinburgh with W A Ramage en route for London. Couldn't get a bus at Barnbougle and took two hours to walk to Barnton for a train. Four busses passed us load[ed] up with sailor men for Edinburgh. Called on Jean and went and booked seats in Theatre Royal for Jean and Billy. Then came off home by N B [North Bridge] to Dalmeny and got a very wet night to come home in. Very tired out.

Friday 9 June 1916

Lay about all day. Got letters from Jim, Lachie and Sandy. They are all well. Bella very hard up.

Saturday 10 June 1916

Went to the doctor for Bella. She is worse this morning. Got my Society money then went to Portobello and saw Aunt Nell. She has been very hard up too. Came home in good time and had to back to the Ferry for medicine for Bella. She's to get rest and a bandage.

Sunday 11 June 1916

Wrote to Sandy, Bob and Lachie. Stayed in the house all day and keept house. Jean went away home on her byke at 12.30 p.m. and got a fine day to run in. Mrs Ramage did not turn up as expected.

Monday June 12 1916

Bella in her bed all day and I head nurse.

Tuesday 13 June 1916

Bella no better. Her leg is less swelled, however.

Wednesday 14 June 1916

Letter from Sandy, Lachie and Bob. Sandy thinks he's going away soon and Lachie is away […].

Thursday 15 June 1916

Jean here today. Her mother is much better of her visit. It cheered her up getting a crack. Wrote to Andrew for his mother.

Friday 16 June 1916

Never was out all day. Only on the hill for firewood.

Saturday 17 June 1916

Saw his old majesty coming up the Hall's brae from the Ferry where he had been seeing the fleet. But, of course, I did not recognise him. Went on to the town after waiting two hours.

Sunday 18 June 1916

Jean here from Edinburgh. She is looking very well. No word of any of the boys since.

Monday 19 June 1916

Very quiet day. No letters. Bella some better.

Tuesday 20 June 1916

Letter of acknowledgement from Lady Clementine Warring to Bella for five shillings sent to her scheme of some sort.

Wednesday 21 June 1916

Bella got a letter from Mrs Stenhouse giving her all the news of what is going on out east. Bella looks and feels much stronger today. David and Imrie her[e] and gave me a cry, en passant.

Thursday 22 June 1916

Went to Edinburgh and got some leather and spriggs for cobbling. Also a [...] drain for emergencies.

Friday 23 June 1916

Went down to the station and got my money and a paper. Called on Davie and Mrs Ramage. Letter from Bob. He is well.

Saturday 24 June 1916

Went to the doctor for a Certificate and came home by the Halls and bought some purchases. Letter from Sandy and Lizzie. Both well.

Sunday 25 June 1916

Very quiet day. Took a walk to the Barbers.

Monday 26 June 1916

Cut an trailed up a big lump of ash and hurt my side. Letter from Andrew.

Tuesday 27 June 1916

Not able to work. Too tired. Took a rest.

Wednesday 28 June 1916

Doctor Dickson here on his motor byke seeing Bella, and refilled her bottle. I went and got it next morning, being too wet to go to the Ferry [today].

Thursday 29 June 1916

Went to the Ferry for medicine. Mr Cassady and a neighbour stuck at the Barbers, coming from Leith.

Friday 30 June 1916

Wet day, very wet day. Peter Robertson and squad cutting down the dirt in the joiner's park.

Saturday 1 July 1916

Big British offensive in France. Big advance over 20 miles. Went to Portobello and saw Nell and Robert. Adam exempted from military service altogether. Got a very wet night coming home. Both very tired. Bella stood it very well. Letter from Willie and Lachie.

Sunday 2 July 1916

Jean and Meg Brand out [and] got a wet day to travel in. Davie's boys, Alick and Erick, up in the afternoon, but did not stay long.

Monday 3 July 1916

Never went far all day. No letters. One from Lizzie.

Tuesday 4 July 1916

[As yesterday]. No letters.

Wednesday 5 July 1916

Letter from Jean, and none from any of the boys.

Thursday 6 July 1916

Lay about all day. Letter from Aunt Lizzie, near Kelso. Very dull wet day. British fighting hard.

Friday 7 July 1916

Very wet day. Expecting Lach[ie] but he never turned up. The Almond [is] in big flood.

Saturday 8 July 1916

Still very wet day. Got a lot of letters today – one from Sandy, Willie and Jamie – all well. Also from Lizzie at Capesthorn. Ella [granddaughter] coming on Monday, she says. Jean came expecting to meet Lach[ie] – who never came.

Sunday 9 July 1916

Jean went away for the five o'clock train. Bella and I went down to the Barbers with her and could hardly get home up the brae.

Monday 10 July 1916

Went to Edinburgh and met Miss Richie at the Waverley and took her to the Rossie place. And then home to Cragie via Forth Brig bus and was very tired when I got up to old Craigie.

Tuesday 11 July 1916

Went to Barnton and saw Miss Richie away to Edinburgh en route for Glasgow. Got a cart of coal.

Wednesday 12 July 1916

Letter from Lach[ie]. He can't get away. The King is going to inspect them on Friday first, so he may get [away] later. Glad to see he was well. No word from Bob yet.

Thursday 13 July 1916

Letter from Bob. He is well and saw James Ramage's regiment en passant but did not know him among the rest. Stayed at home all day.

Friday 14 July 1916
Day at home. Took a walk with Ella.

Saturday 15 July 1916
Saint Swithin's Day. Some rain so we are in for it for another six weeks. Ella and I at Queensferry and called on D and Mrs Ramage, at Dalmeny.

Sunday 16 July 1916
Jean here from Edinburgh.

Monday 17 July 1916
Lachie from Chelmsford.

Tuesday 18 July 1916
Lachie and I at Portobello. Aunt Nell's birthday. Boswell's fair day. Saw Adam home from Berwick.

Wednesday 19 July 1916
Lachie at Leith seeing Mr Cassiday. Late of being home.

Thursday 20 July 1916
Lachie at Edinburgh, but came home with Jean and saw her back to Barnton.

Friday 21 July 1916
Went and saw Lachie away at Waverly Station, Edinburgh. Jean came down with sausage for him.

Saturday 22 July 1916
Went to Edinburgh and Portobello and got my pay. My watch not ready yet – not for another fortnight.

Sunday 23 July 1916
Wrote to Sandy and Willie. They are both well. Bill is back at Alexandria and he is having a good time.

Monday 24 July 1916
Very quiet day. Nothing doing. Letter from Sandy from the Front.

Tuesday 25 July 1916
Nothing doing. Postcard from Sandy.

Wednesday 26 July 1916
Do. Do. [Ditto Ditto].

Thursday 27 July 1916
Do. Do. [Ditto Ditto].

Tuesday 1 August 1916 –

Friday 11 August 1916
Letter[s] from Sandy and Willie. Both Well. Willie back to Salonika. Letter from W A Ramage, London on Tuesday this week. Jean and Ella away to Linton today. It's very foggy.

Saturday 12 August 1916
No grouse shooting today. Everything quiet on the moors. Jean away to Dunfermline to see Mrs Balfour and Miss Heart.

Sunday 13 August 1916
Jean at Dunfermline for a weekend with Beth.

Monday 14 August 1916
Forgot Bella's letter so I went down to Dalmeny and posted [it]. Saw Polly gathering up man's bonnet in the cornfield and [she]

hid it in the machine shed. Man up from Carlwine at night seeking it, and young miss came down and opened the door for him to get in for it.

Tuesday 15 Augt 1916

Jamie Darling's sister arrove from Cockburnspath. Davie came up with Jean last night. He was going to Carlowrie. No fuss here tonight, all quiet.

Wednesday 16 August 1916

Went to Dalmeny and ordered my passes for Manchester for the 26th inst. Came up by David and got my tea along with him.

Thursday 17 August 1916

Davie and Imrie at midday. Jean at Golf Hall seeing Mary Woudger. I met her at foot of the brae – she was on her byke.

Thursday 17 August 1916

Very little doing here.

Friday 18 August 1916

Letter from Willie from Salonika. He is up at the Front at Lake Doiran. French troops engaged. Jean and Ella away to Edinburgh, perhaps to call on Mrs McDonald [Sandy's mother-in-law]. Mrs Muirhead at Lowood. The two cycling young ladies very busy tonight.

Saturday 19 August 1916

Went to the doctor and got leave to take change of air. Got my pension. Letter[s] from Lachie, and Flo, and from Bob. Both well. No word from Jim.

Sunday 20 August 1916

Went to church with Jean and Ella. David not able to work yet.

Two boys up. Jean, Ella and I went down to the sea via Dalmeny Home Farm, and got some rain coming home.

Monday 21 August 1916

Letter from Jamie. He is well. Wrote to Willie and Lachie. Jean at the Post Office with letters, and postcard to Mrs McDonald.

Tuesday 22 August 1916

Went to Edinburgh and saw Jean away to Newhall. Called with Ella on her Rossie Place Granny.

Wednesday 23 August 1916

Had a good day's rest. Lay about all day. Wrote to Nell, and Bob, and Jim.

Thursday 24 August 1916

Went over the Forth Bridge with Ella, just to let her see it before she left for home. It was a bit misty and no view going. Went and got my passes from Mr Wilson at Dalmeny, and went down to South Queensferry for an errand for Bella and called on Davie, en passant. No letters.

Friday 25 August 1916

Got a letter from Sandy. He is well. Wrote to him, and Ella added a few lines to send away in the morning. Very wet, dis-agreeble day. Hardly ever out all day. If [it] is God's will, we will leave for Capesthorn in the morning by the 8.54 a.m.

Saturday 26 August 1916

Made a safe journey to Capesthorn. Old Mr Carrie met us at Chelford and drove us up. We were all very tired but found Lizzie and the boys all right.

Sunday 27 August 1916
Lay about all day, tired.

Monday 28 August 1916

Took a walk about and renewed old acquaintance with all the estate folks.

Tuesday 29 August 1916

Took a turn with Carrie, rabbit catching among the harvesters.

Wednesday 30 August 1916

Took a walk up to the Post Office for letters, but got none.

Thursday 31 August 1916

Bella and I enjoying ourself. I'm sawing sticks and she's looking after the bairns.

Friday 1 September 1916

Was at Macclesfield on Saturday, with Lizzie in the bus. Had to stand all the way home, nearly. Sunday very quiet. Got my letters and money all right, and I've next went to the Carrie's and had our tea and spent the night in music on Monday and I kept cutting sticks all the next day. Took the byke and ran in to Macclesfield and bought a silk blouse for Jean and a waisecoat to myself (Tuesday).

Wednesday 6 September 1916

Was invited by Mrs W Bromley-Davenport to tea in the Hall and to see through the house. So we had a rare night.

Thursday 7 September 1916

Went to Alderley Edge with Lizzie on our bykes. Pretty rough road. Went and had tea with Mr and Mrs Dewar and had a look through the garden, etc.

Friday 8 September 1916

Travelled home to Craigie all right and got on fine, but was very tired.

Saturday 9 September 1916
Lay about all day and took a rest.

Sunday 10 September 1916
Do. Do. [Ditto Ditto].

Monday 11, Tuesday 12, Wednesday 13 September 1916
Nothing doing here.

Thursday 14 September 1916
Wrote to Bob and sent him some socks and sweets. Also Willie and Lachie.

Friday 15 September 1916
Thirty two years[96] since I got my arm taken off, and it passed away very quietly. Went to Gogar.

Saturday 16 September 1916
Went down to Dalmeny and drew my pension and called on David en route. And [then] spent the day very quietly at home.

Sunday 17 September 1916
Took a walk with Mr McDermid, round by Burnfoot and home. Bella and I took a walk round the wood and spent the evening quietly.

Monday 18 September 1916
No word from any of the boys.

Tuesday 19 September 1916
No letters from any of the boys yet.

Wednesday 20 September 1916
Letter from Sandy and Lizzie. They are both well.

Thursday 21 September 1916

Letter from Lachie, and another from the Pay Master General, Ripon. Lachie is all right and The Pay Master wants to know if Bella can't do with a smaller allowance from the government.

Friday 22 September 1916

Letter from Bobie. He is back to the sheds again. Wonder what's gone wrong? But he likes it better – says it's like old times. Ian Grearson is a sergeant now. He has seen him. Henderson stacking corn out in front of our house. Miss Glendinning up here with turnips and onions for us.

Saturday 23 September 1916

Went to Portobello and saw Aunt Nell. Both she and Bob are very hard up and Adam has been called up by the military for General Service. So she is worrying about that too. Got home at seven o'clock. Someone from Dalmeny here in our absence.

Sunday 24 September 1916

Very quiet day. Took a walk down by Burnshot and Barnbougle. Met Mr and Mrs Darling at Sander's road end and got away to bed in good time.

Monday 25 September 1916

Very quiet day again. Got a postcard from Sandy – so he is all right. Also a letter from Lizzie. Wrote all the boys but Jamie.

Tuesday 26 September 1916

Did not write to the above ad[vertisement]. Thought better. Bella went to Cramond Brig and brought home her money. Afraid to put it away. I keept house till she came home. Everything very quiet.

Wednesday 27 September 1916

Very quiet. Nothing doing but gathering sticks.

Thursday 28 September 1916
Cutting sticks and brambles.

Friday 29 September 1916

Letters from Lachie and Jean. Went to the Ferry and was too late for the doctor. Got my pension money etc, and other things from the Ferry – but no sugar. Went to Kirkliston on the same errand, but was unsuccessfull there too.

Saturday 30 September 1916

Went to Edinburgh and got my Guards' Society money and four pounds brown sugar from Law & Forrest, Queensferry Station. Got a letter from Willie. He has been in the trenches and was out for a spell.

Sunday 1 October 1916

Went down to the Post Office but no letters. Bella and I took a walk round Craigie Hill. I pulled some brambles later. Very quiet day. Zep[pelin] brought down near Lon[don].

Monday 2 October 1916

Went to the doctor and got a Certificate and posted it there, but made a botch of the signature. Old Henderson with his men all day chasing them on with leaving some of his wheat stacks […]ing like a […] and will need to come doon again. No berries to be got but red ones.

Tuesday 3 October 1916

Wet day. Got some brambles, but got wet too. The lights are going same as usual. No letters.

Wednesday 4 October 1916
No letters yet.

Thursday 5 October 1916 –

Monday 16 October 1916

Letters from Aunt Nell and Lachie. All well at Portobello and Lachie is the same, but wearying.

Tuesday 17 October 1916

Letter from Bob at last. It was a weary wait, but he is alright, so that's everything.

Wednesday 18 October 1916

Sent away a letter to Sandy and Bob but keipt back Jamie's as I got one from him so wanted to see his news. He is well and very quiet. Had a big day cutting sticks and cutting them up.

Thursday 19 October 1916

Bella got a letter from Mrs Stenhouse with all her news, and we had another big day cutting and carrying wood from Carlowrie Hill. Shepherd came to stay with Mrs Muirhead for the […].

Friday 20 October 1916

Big day at the wood. Letter from Lachie.

Saturday 21 October 1916

Went to Edinburgh and saw Jean and had a big afternoon. Got home in beautiful searchlights.

Sunday 22 October 1916

Went to church and Davie came up to Dolphinton with us. Lay about all day after.

Monday 23 October 1916

Cut some fir and carried it home. Stiff job. Mrs Muirhead at Edinburgh.

Tuesday 24 October 1916

Letter from Sandy. He is all right and getting on fine. Couldn't get to the wood as Lord Rosebery was out shooting.

Wednesday 25 October 1916

No sticks. Shooting still going on. Poor Angus wrote his last letter to us two years ago. Mrs Muirhead at Edinburgh. No letters from anyone yet.

Thursday 26 October 1916

Angus killed on [this date] 1914. Poor Angus. Jean and her cook came out in the bus and went home in the train.

Friday 27 October 1916

Went to the station and doctor and got a Certificate and home at eleven o'clock. Bella got a letter from Mrs McDonald, Cross Keys. W Hope got his leg broken at the shooting. Rows at Craigie with Mickle and old Henderson. Saw old Birnie going to the doctor this morning.

Saturday 28 October 1916

Went to Portobello and saw Aunt Nell. She is very hard up today and so is Rab – he'd lay in bed all day. Got home in good time, before six o'clock.

Sunday 29 October 1916

Lachie's birthday, so I wrote him a letter and sent him some postcards. Wet all afternoon so we stayed in the house.

Monday 30 October 1916

No letters from Willie yet. Letter from Jean and Lachie with postcard enclosed. He is well but back in the D Company again. Took a walk round by Lowood and the smithy. Saw James Darling with the smithy man and four Irishmen building up drystone dykes. Lousy lot at thirty five shillings per week.

Tuesday 31 October 1916

Lay about all afternoon and took a walk after tea.

Wednesday 1 November 1916

Letter from Lachie. He is alright and going to get home soon to see us. So he will be going to the Front in France soon. So he'll be the last of five sons. Poor Lachie, hope he has good luck.

Thursday 2 November 1916

Letter from Bob at last. He is well (thank God for His loving kindness). Went to Kirkliston and got a bottle of aqua[97] and home in two hours.

Friday 3 November 1916

Field card from Sandy.[98] He is well and thank God, from whom all blessings flow. Big forenoon sawing sticks, and lay about all afternoon. Irish tattie workers idle.

Saturday 4 November 1916

Took a walk in the afternoon to the Ferry and had a sair struggle to get home. Very tired.

Sunday 5 November 1916.

Never left the ho[use]. Very wet day. Wee Davie up from Dalmeny. Wrote to all my folks.

Monday 6 November 1916

Letter from Aunt Nell and Jamie. He is going to be shifted to Salonika. He has applied for a shift. So I wrote by return post. Also a letter from Jean. She is in bed with a cold, but getting better. Also a letter from Mary Jane McLean inviting us both to Selkirk.

Tuesday 7 November 1916

Few lines from Willie. He is in No. 5 Canadian Hospital,

Salonika, with malarial fever, poor soul, but getting better.[99] So I wrote off to him at once, and also to Aunt Nell saying where he was.

Wednesday 8 November 1916

Letter from Sandy's wife telling us she had a letter from Willie. They are all well at Capesthorn so Bella sent her a postcard. The tatties [are] all up, and all the Irish going away tomorrow.

Thursday 9 November 1916

Got a letter from Sandy. He is getting on fine and very busy. We had Jean out and she is all clear of her cold again. So Bella and I went down to Burnshot and saw her on her way away home. Irish tattie gatherers away home to Oirland, all but a few.

Friday 10 November 1916

Another letter from Willie. He is getting out of hospital for a convalescence for a few days – before returning to his regiment. Took a walk down to half[way] between Barnbougle and Burnshot and mended my byke after.

Saturday 11 November 1916

Went to Dalmeny Station and Queensferry for Doctor's Certificate. After dinner cycled to Edinburgh and left my byke at Jean's and did my business and cycled back against a head wind. [I] was very nearly worn out before I got home. Lost my hat.

Sunday 12 November 1916

Went to church and got a good sermon from Mr Dun[n] and called on Davie coming home and spent a very quiet evening.

Monday 13 November 1916

The tattie lifters away home to Oirland. May they never leave it.

Tuesday 14 November 1916

Had old Dan in playing draughts. Went down to the Post Office with Bella and walked up the river side coming home and had a look through the Grotto.

Wednesday 15 November 1916

Took a walk round the quarry and saw a nest of bullfinches – very bonny ones too. Lay about all day. Got a field card from Bob. He is well – will write later.

Thursday 16 November 1916

Went to Edinburgh with socks to Jean to send off to Willie and Jamie for their Christmas parcels – which she is to make up and send on. Bought a watch chain and got a braw one from Jean. So I'm well chained now. Some tattie stealing going on up to the old stable, so there will be a row soon.

Friday 17 November 1916

Got Bob's promised letter. He is well but bust, poor chap.

Saturday 18 November 1916

Very wet. Lachie arrove by the fast train to Barnton from Edinburgh. He travelled all night from Chelmsford, and we lay about day.

Sunday 19 November 1916

Jean came in all the rain to see Lachie and he went down to Barnton Station and saw her away home by the last train. Very wet day – so I stayed in the house all day.

Monday 20 November 1916

Lachie went to see Jean and Mrs Cassiday at Leith, and got a wet day. Davie was here when he came home.

Tuesday 21 November 1916

Went to Edinburgh with Lachie and got his photo taken with him, and him taken by himself – and [then] came home all right. Lachie got a wristlet watch.

Wednesday 22 November 1916

Went to the Waverly Station and saw Lachie away home to his regiment again. It's just like parting with them altogether, but he went off quite cheery. We then ran down and saw our Aunt Nell at Portobello. They are much better, but hard up still. Called on Jean and found her well, but sad about Lachie.

Thursday 23 November 1916

Another wet day. Went and brought some sticks, and cut them up and lay about all day.

Friday 24 November 1916

Went to Edinburgh and got my new breeks and silk vest fitted on at the Co-op. Then to Edinburgh and Waverly Station and got my Guards' money and home in good time.

Saturday 25 November 1916

Went to the Ferry to Dr Dickson and got a Certificate. Came home by Dalmeny and called on D Ramage. They are all well. The misses was bursting with news.

Sunday 26 November 1916

Bella and I went to Dalmeny Church and called on David, but he was out at the station. Some one lifting goods. Lay about all afternoon, and wrote a letter to Jamie.

Monday 27 November 1916

Bella washing. I carried some sticks and went down with an answer to Sandy's letter we got this morning. Sent away some bacca and a pipe to Jamie.

Tuesday 28 November 1916
Don't remember ought.

Wednesday 29, Thursday 30 November 1916
    Small tray
    Delf basin.
    Zink pail and bath
    Fork and ladle
    [...] cover

Friday 1 December 1915
No word from any of the boys. Very dull.

Saturday 2 December 1916
Still no letters from any of the boys. Went to Leith for fish –
walked in.

Sunday 3 December 1916
Still no letters. Went to the Post Office in vain. Jamie Darling
away east at North Berwick.

Monday 4 December 1916
Still no letters.

Tuesday 5 December 1916
Went to Post Office with Bella and met Phemie and James
Kinnear [niece and nephew], who had been at our house and
turned back with us and got the bus from Barnbougle Gate.
James looks well in his highland costume. Went to Edinburgh
for photos.

Wednesday 6 December 1916
Never carried sticks all day – too tired.

Thursday 7 December 1916

Jean here from Edinburgh. Great rows in parliament. Letter from the War Office.

Friday 8 December 1916

Went and saw the doctor. Called on David and got him to come up and cut my hair.

Saturday 9 December 1916

Had to go back to the doctor with my paper as he signed the wrong certificate for me. He was gey snotty. Very wet day. Letter from _ . No letters War Office.

Sunday 10 December 1916

Went to Cramond Brig. No letters. Wrote to all the boys but Lachie. Bella wrote to Lizzie. No church. Wet day.

Monday 11 December 1916

Letter from Nell. All in their ordinary way. Lay about all day, shivery and cold.

Tuesday 12 December 1916

Bella and I went to Edinburgh and bought a lot of furniture, etc. Called on Jean and got home at 4.00 p.m. Very wet day and very tired.

Wednesday 13 December 1916

The grocer's van only brought the bread, and nothing else we bought.

Thursday 14 December 1916

Making things ready for our lodgers coming.

Friday 15 December 1916

The Rev Mr Evans and wife arrove in a Ha[ll] cab at seven forty-five. Very tired. No letters.

Saturday 16 December 1916

Went to Edinburgh and bought some goods for our visitors, coming tomorrow from Edinburgh. No word from the boys.

Sunday 17 December 1916

No letters today. Only a paper to Mrs Evans. The Rev gentlman got to his ship, but came home again. Lay in the house all day.

Monday 18 December 1916

No letters yet. Mr Evans on board again. He got a supply of mutton and so he is all right again. Got the things from Co-op.

Tuesday 19 December 1916

No letters, only *Courier* paper. Went to Post Office with Bella and got my first payment for Jamie, poor Chap. Wish I got a few lines from him.

Wednesday 20 December 1916

Home company.

Thursday 21 December 1916

Shortest day. Got a present each from Lachie. A row about taties stealing. Old Henderson moving.

Friday 22 December 1916

Went and saw the doctor and paid his account − nine shillings − and got Doctor's Certificate and some powders. Took a walk through the Ferry and up the steps to the station for pension, six shillings. Called on Davie going home.

Saturday 23 December 1916

Went to Edinburgh and Portobello. Called on Jean and Aunt Nell and dined with them both. Got on alright. Letter from Sandy and Bob – both well.

Sunday 24 December 1916

No letters. No Kirkin. Took a walk down to Dalmeny. Man killed in the mine. Had Alick and the young smith, Mr Evans and his wife on board for Christmas.

Monday 25 December 1916

Christmas day very quiet up here. Mrs Ramage up and got her tea with us here – the only one we saw. Letters from Jamie, both very late.

Tuesday 26 December 1916

Went down to the Post Office with Bella for her pay.

Wednesday 27 December 1916

Very quiet day.

Thursday 28 December 1916

Do. [Ditto].

Friday 29 December 1916

Went to Kirkliston for my New Year's bottle, etc.

Saturday 30 December 1916

Went to Edinburgh and called on Jean and got her out shopping for me, and got my two cheques cashed at the Store.

Sunday 31 December 1916

Went to church and came home with Dan. Got a good sermon.

Monday 1 January 1917

New Year's day. Went down and had my New Year's dinner
at Dalmeny with Davie and family, and everything passed off
alright.

Tuesday 2 January 1917

Got a letter from Miss Ritchie and Andrew – who has come out
alright. £187 for 1,400 bushels of wheat, and some left over for
seed and feed. No word from Lachie, or any of Sandy's folk.
Something wrong.

Wednesday 3 January 1917

Carrying sticks and sawing them up.

Thursday 4 January 1917

Another quiet day. No letter.

Friday 5 January 1917

Letters from both Sandy and Bob. They are well and had a
cheery Christmas and New Year, but no leave for them.

Saturday 6 January 1917

Went to the Ferry and got my Doctor's Certificate. He was trying to dish me again, but put it off with an oily laugh. Went to
Edinburgh [in the] afternoon. Called on Flory [Florrie] for an
hour.

Sunday 7 January 1917

Went down to the Post Office. No letters today. Dog howled at
Wheatland. Hope there's nought wrong.

Monday 8 January 1917

No letters. Stayed at home all day. Very dull.

Tuesday 9 January 1917
Do. Do. Do. [Ditto Ditto Ditto].

Wednesday 10 January 1917
Do. Do. Do. Do. [Ditto Ditto Ditto Ditto].

Thursday 11 January 1917
Still no letters. Wrote to Lachie.

Friday 12 January 1917
Letters from Lachie so I keipt back mine till I got his news. He forgot to post his last letter so he sent them both off at once. He is alright and bound for Ireland.

Saturday 13 January 1917
Went to Edinburgh and banked £5 with the Railway Company's Savings Bank. Called on Jean. Sent off an answer to Lachie. Came and went by the buss, no train at eleven twenty-five.

Sunday 14 January 1917
No church today. Too cold. Jean and Katie Russel[l] from Charlotte Square – had to walk home in a snowstorm. Got home at 9.30. p.m. alright.

Monday 15 January 1917
Went to see Aunt Nell and found all well. Saw Checker's funeral – [he] was killed in the yard – got both his legs run over. Got a letter from Jim.

Tuesday 16 January 1917
Very quiet day. Nothing doing.

Wednesday 17 January 1917 –
Thursday 18 January 1917 –

Friday 19 January 1917

Went down to the doctor but he was not to be in till 2.30 p.m.
Letters from Sandy and Willie, and postcard [from] Bob.

Saturday 20 January 1917

Went and saw doctor and went to Edinburgh by train and dined
with Jean and A_ .

Sunday 21 January 1917

Never went far from the door. Too cold to go to the Post Office
even. Never saw any of Davie's folks.

Monday 22 January 1917

Very quiet day. Not very strong. Never did anything but lay
about all day.

Tuesday 23 January 1917

Went to the Post Office with Bella. Very quiet day. Letter from
Lachie, from Dublin. Sent away a reply.

Wednesday 24 January 1917

Letter from Jamie. He got my parcel with pipe and bacca and
replied at once. He is well. Mr Evans off duty today. They were
standing ready yesterday. Been a naval scrap in the North Sea
with the Zeebrugge flotilla, and according to reports the
German huns caught a tarter.

Thursday 25 January 1917

　　Burns' birthday.

　　　　O wad some poor the gift tae ge us
　　　　To see ourselves as others see us
　　　　It wad frae mony a blunder frae us
　　　　What airs in dress and gate wad free us
　　　　And ever return.

Friday 26 January 1917

The chaplain and his wife awa to Edinburgh. His boat no [movin] the day and so he's payin a holiday. Sandy's parcel returned – wrong adressed and aa the goods destroyed wi carbolic soap and trench powder.

Saturday 27 January 1917

Went to Edinburgh and got [...]. Couldnae get any fish. Herring threepence each. So called on Jean and came home wi the bus.

Sunday 28 January 1917

Very quiet day. Two of Davie's boys up calling on us. They are all well at home. Jamie wrote thanking the minister.

Monday 29 January 1917

Mr Evans leaving on Wednesday with his wife. He will see her away from the Waverly Station for home, as his ship sails on Thursday for foreign parts. Letter from Lachie, needing a shirt. Enclosed ten shillings for his mother to buy him one.

Tuesday 30 January 1917

Wrote to Lachie and Aunt Nell and lay about all day. Henderson got in the mill to thrash and bunch. Letter from Jean.

Wednesday 31 January 1917

Letter from Willie. He is on out-post duty, attached to an infantry regiment about seven miles from his own squadron. Mr and Mrs Evans left here at 12.15 for Dalmeny Station – thence to Edinburgh where he parted with her, returning here and got tea with us in the kitchen before going on board to sail tomorrow. I wish both he and his wife good luck. They were quite nice lodgers. They were laith [loath] to part and gang away.

Thursday 1 February 1917

Jean here today. Mr Evans would leave the Ferry – sea to thick to see his ship pass. First day of German piracy and ruthlesness will be wigs on the green.[100] Gentleman with a byke seeking Carlowrie, a cockney with plenty gas. Old Henderson busy working himself at the hay baling, so he must be in a hurry.

Friday 2 February 1917

No word from any of the boys. Went to Portobello and saw Aunt Nell. Adam fu – he's on the young beef.

Saturday 3 February 1917

Went to the doctor, the station, and called on D Ramage who came up to Dolphinton. After dinner, took a walk round the triangle. Got a letter from Lachie. He is well and still in Dublin city.

Sunday 4 February 1917

Went down to Post Office. No letters. Had a call off David, and Mrs Ramage to tea. Went over to Dudgeons going home.

Monday 5 February 1917
Very quiet day. No letters.

Tuesday 6 February 1917
Letter from George. He tells us all about his wheat failure, etc.

Wednesday 7 February 1917
No letter from Bob yet. Wonder what's wrong with him?

Thursday 8 February 1917
What's wrong with everything? I'm so sad I can't get my spirits up. No letters yet. Went to Edinburgh with Bella.

Friday 9 February 1917
Letter from Sandy and Jim. Both well. Also a demand from Leuchold for £5.00 for rent. Went over and paid it at once, to

Bore, the clerk. Can't say out about the house rent or out else. Only going to see.

Saturday 10 February 1917

Walked to leith on a tour, but was very tired when I got home with half a dozen herring for my Sunday's breakfast. No letters today.

Sunday 11 February 1917

Walked to the Post Office and got a letter from Jim and Sandy. Both well. Sandy sent a postcard – photo taken on a motor byke. He looks all right and they are both well.

Monday 12 February 1917

Made up two parcels for Jim and Willie, Salonika force, to send away tomorrow when we go to the Post Office at [Cramond Brig].

Tuesday 13 February 1917

Got a letter from Lachie and a postcard from Sandy yesterday. Went down with Bella and sent the boys parcels to Salonika. Very frosty day. Bella very tired walking both up and down. Saw Miss Jane and Miss Dudgeon – cadging for the church.

Wednesday 14 February 1917

Letter from Lachie. He got his parcel all right and is getting on fine but it is gey and cauld in Dublin. Had a visit off Davie, en passant to the choir. They are all well at Dalmeny and Kelso.

Thursday 15 February 1917

Letters from Aunt Nell and Sandy. Nell was wishing me many returns of my birthday. This is my sixty-third, now I'm getting on. Bella and I went to Edinburgh to her dressmaker and she called on Jean who had been two days off duty with the flu. I went to my watch maker and got a new glass in my watch. Waiting on Davy to cut my hair.

Friday 16 February 1917

Went to the doctor and also drew my pension, en passant. Called on Mrs Ramage, and Davie came round to Dolphinton with me on his way to the house.

Saturday 17 February 1917, Sunday 18 February 1917 –

Monday 19 February 1917

Lay about all week. Not so well. A bit tired and lazy, I think.

Tuesday 20 February 1917

Letter from Sandy. He is well. No word from any of the rest of the boys.

Wednesday 21 February 1917

Letter and photo from Lachie, from Dublin. He looks thin, but says he is keeping better.

Thursday 22 February 1917

Had Maggie Brand [here] and went down to Burnshot with her and saw her into the carr[iage]. Very dark going down [there].

Friday 23 February 1917

Letter from Aunt Lizzie. They are stoppin on again at nine shilling of a rise [increase] for the two. David cut my hair and brought up a bit colman or sea salmon. Letter from Andrew.

Saturday 24 February 1917

Went to Leith to see a Mr Reid about a place at Samuelston, Loanhead.

Sunday 25 February 1917

Wrote to Sandy, Andrew and Lachie. Not very well today.

Thursday 15 March 1917
Went to Greenside to Tabs Stores and sent away a half pound of bacca to Jamie, to Salonika.

Friday 16 March 1917
Lay about all day. Too cold to go to the Ferry.

Saturday 17 March 1917
Went to Portobello and saw Nell and Robert and got my money at the Waverly Station. Came and went by the motor carr[iage].

Sunday 18 March 1917
Went to the Post Office but got nothing. Took a walk to Carlowrie after dinner with […].

Monday 19 March 1917
Went to the doctors at [Queens]ferry and got a certificate from the doctor.

Saturday 31 March 1917
Went to Edinburgh and saw Jean and Kitty going to a Highland Fair. And heard the band playing on George Street and another, in scarlet coats, marching through the street – beating up subscribers.

Sunday 1 April 1917
Got a postcard from Lachie. Took a walk to the airodrome at Turnhouse, to [see] the planes flying. Came home by Craigiehall with Bella. Met Maggie Muirhead and Johnie Liberton on route. Wrote to Jamie. Had three of Davie's kids and two strangers waiting on us for tea, and kids had the wagonette out running about all afternoon.

Thursday 17 May 1917
Wrote Jim and Lachie. No letters from anyone. Lay about all day. Very sad reading in the *Scotsman*.

Saturday 9 June 1917

Lachie arove from Dublin, looking well, on four days leave.
Had a trip to Edinburgh after dinner.

Wednesday 13 June 1917

Went to Dalmeny and saw Lachie away to Dublin, via Belfast.
Sad parting.

Thursday 21 June 1917

Postcard from Lachie. He is at Folkestone, and quite cheery.
Waiting to cross to France. Letter from Kitty Russel. No word
from any of the boys from abroad. *AR*.

* * *

(Left to right) Lauchlan (Lachie), Andrew, Anna Moore,
Jim, Bella, Dod and Jean, at Dalmeny, 1929.

DIARY

Entries extracted
from Parts I and II

Diary entry for Monday, 31 December 1888

Mr Editor

Once more Farmer's Son enlightens us as to how we are to better our selves and families. Without asking an advance of wages from his father – or mother as the case may be – I wonder what he or his parents would think of their landlord [if], on being approached for a reduction of rent, was to turn round and say, 'Why? You are very well off. I see you can keep (say) two or perhaps three idle horses for your family to sport about the country. Or a liveried servant to drive your self and wife about, and a governess to educate and be a mother to [your children]. Now, Mr So-and-so, allow me to point out to you that if you would keep your self at your proper level – as a farmer – instead of imitating your landlord [...]. Put away your useles horses and servants. Make your family work, and work yourselves. And give [up] your pipe and brandy bottle. No more visiting about the country, no more expensive dinners, etc. and you will easily pay your preasent rent and give your men a reasonable wage and stop their applying to parliament for [redress]. Give them either a money wage or boll, whichever they want, and let us hear no more about your giving your servants boll when the markets are low, and whenever they rise giving them money. There tricks are dishonourable and will have to be stopped or [...]. So, at the end of your lease now, this is the advice Farmer's Son gives to ploughmen. They don't require any more wages. You have 23£, and your gains.[101] *You have one pound per month to pay your groceries. And meal and potatoes of your own which, if you were not too nice to use, you would be very comfortable. You have a pig to keep your house in kitchen, your coals driven and a free house. With the rest of your wages paid half-yearly when you can* [then] *pay your tailor and shoemaker. I consider you are very well off. Learn your brats and bairns to eat the barley we give you, instead of feeding your pig on it. Give them oatmeal twice a day, and take the same yourself, and I don't see what more you would like. He has got to learn that a poor man can keep his family cheaper on tea and loaf bread than on poridge and milk. Another thing I would like to suggest to this milk and water puppet – as the guid wife in Berwickshire stiles him – is that* [were] *his father* [to give] *him a pair of horses to drive at 14s per week, and one of his sisters to keep house for him for an year,* [...] *I have no doubt he would have more sympathy with ploughmen next year*

Diary entry for 11 January 1889

Stenton Gates

Mr Editor

Sir, I am a constant reader of your valuable paper and, if I may claim a portion of that space, I have followed the ploughmans' controversy with much interest, being an old hind myself. Your correspondent, Far East, not content to stick to his point and discuss the wages of ploughmen, must neads start off on a fresh tack, as they say about Dunbar. Being boted into a corner by the ploughman from Longniddry – who is aparently a man of experience who can prove what he says – I wonder what good he will get from making a comparison between railwaymen and ploughmen. Or, if he only wants information, he must be very ignorant indeed if he does not know that. Ploughmen think themselves highly favoiured if they should succeed in getting an appointment on any of our railways. Say begining at the lowest three grades at 16s weekly, as an engine cleaner, with his turn of promotion as a foreman and then as a driver, or as a porter, at 19[s], with his chance of promotion in that department. Or again, as a sur-faceman, at 17s. Here you find most ploughmen, and most all of them the best in their district – married men with families who prefer remaining in the country to going to town. The young men nearly all prefer the other two branches. Well, let Far East try any of those men, and see how many of them would go back to the plough. Not only from the railway, but the police, the tramway – or even – from the police dung carts. I never yet knew a man in any of these positions, unless indeed he was force to leave them through his own bad behaviour and saw nothing staring him in the face but starvation, who would leave them and go back to be a farmservant. In any of the other [positions] he may attain he feels he is a man, and is respected according as he be-haves himself. But as a farmservant, he is treated with contempt by such milk and water puppits – as the ploughman's quid wife termed them. And Far East and Farmer's Son would do well to take a year or two at the [plough] themselves before they take up the cudgels against the men whose toil upholds their glitter-ing show, and who they view as creatures of another kind – fit only to be scoffed at when they make an honest attempt to form an association with the object of raiseing themselves out of the slough of dispondency in which they sink and which will do far more for them than either the Kirk or the Sunday School would [do]. As you [get] little there in the ways of information, except […] go there with the intention [to] view it as in a theatrical light. So, you can study the airs and graces and piouse proud faces of the very class who advise you to come to church – especially the younger generation. What will they learn? Nothing. What will they see? Spite and envy. If you had seen them, as I have done, after coming from the Lord's Sacrament, chasing a w_ [woman] through the by-paths like a b_, you would not be surprised to know that ploughmen prefer to keep their children at home rather than approach the house of God in such un-Godly company. As I said before, if they would work, as some of them profess to, instead of lo[af]ing about after a few workers [and] while they make old men work hard for next to nothing. By beginning at the bottom of the ladder, instead of looking down from the top, they would perhaps [gain] a different view. But they find it more congennial to stand with a hoe under there arm – or perhaps, as they are otherwise inclined, they may stay at home and chase the maid round the steading like a country cousin, till she has either to give in or leave her place in disgrace in the middle of her term. For, of course, if she makes a complaint she is condemned herself. She must have given him incouragement, etc. One little Irish girl I knew was annoyed by one of those contemptable church going currs, but was one too many for him. She tripped him up and slapped his ears and threatened to tell his father, till the blubbly Jack whinged and cried like a child for fear he might be put out of the [choir] if it got abroad. And the next poor woman who came, not having the same spirit, ran away rather than sufer the annoyance. These are exceptional instances I must own, but when you see such scoundrells setting up there own as would-be leaders of public opinion, one cannot help attack them. There are seven or eight in this locality. I could name farmer's sons the most drunken and debauched fellows you could get in a day's travel among plough men. So, now I think I have had my fling. Only, I would advise Far East to try [to] disprove what the ploughman says about the stand[ards] and wages in the country, and if he finds he has reckoned without his host, let him sing dumb or own up like a man, and not deal in gibes and snears about hope bitters. If I am not mistaken, he is likelier to turn out a patent medicine vendor[102] than a farmer competent to speak on the wages question. But this I may say – that the more strenious his and other opposition to the ploughmen's cause, the more sensible, enlightened men will be attracted to their cause. And in spite of them, we will yet see plough men and their families worthily filling the honourable positions of farmers, and their families working to support them – instead of spending their means, and making their lives miserable and their farms failiures, as at present. I am, Mr Editor, a railway man and friend of the ploughmen.

Yours faithfully

Andrew Ramage

Mr Editor

*If I may claim a space in your valuable paper with a few remarks
on the ploughmans' controversy, which I have followed with
much interest. I am glad to see that in spite of all opposition the
ploughmen's cause has been expoused by some sensible practable
men who, instead of trying to tie them down, are pointing out
the way. There are plenty of men I know who have grown up
families, very badly employed, who could find employment for
them on a small holding or croft. And to those men I say, now is
your chance. Strike while the iron is hot. Mr Haldane, tells you
plainly the money will be forthcoming – only let the right men
come forward. The opposition of Farmer's Son and Far East has
already born good fruit, as they might have known, as showing
the general public what sort of help they were likely to get from
their employers or their sons. Nothing but vituperative ridicule,
I think. Somebody has been knocking this into farmers sons, for
they are keeping discreetly silent – all of them – but Far East. And
he, being beaten compleetly by the child frae Langniddry, has
now given it up and made some sneering comment avent hope
bitters. This, I believe, to be liker his occupation than a farmer.
He very possibly gets his livery by vending patent medicines and
could not miss this chance of saying a word for his hopes. You
see, he says mutton is no go – so he can't be a butcher. As to
potatoes being better tasted by hope manners, that wants to be
demonstrated yet. So he finishes up by wanting some information
about railway men's wages. Well, I think it would be a pity if
Ploughman gave him any information on the subject as possibly
it may do a great deal of harm to him, unintentional – of course
– on the ploughman's part, but not so on the part of Far East as
quite possibly he may have a few miserable shares. And, when he
finds that the railway man is better off than the ploughman, he
may make a motion at the next half-yearly meeting of directors to
reduce them a shilling to bring them on a level with the ploughmen and others. There is only one farmer in East Lothian who
pays his men at or over what the surfacemen have, and then
when you take into consideration the half-day on Saturday and*

no work on Sunday, or after dusk in winter, I do not think you will get one old ploughman between Berwick and Edinburgh, and they are nearly all so, who would go to him from the railway – although he is a gentleman in word and deed and knows when a man works a day's work without standing over him, [or] growl in at him every time he sits. Just fancy a railway servant going to leave the railway and return to a farmer for 23£ in money and his miserable gains. One would think he could pay a house rent and takes off his preasent and have a few pounds a year to the good, unless in cases of sickness. Here, again, he is more faviourably placed than Ploughman – for having an extra shilling or two, he can invest in a society which provides for this. I am one old ploughman now on the railway in one of the lowest grades and I would not exchange with the majority of them at present. Let us hope this will not long continue and that better days are at hand. Meanwhile, I remain, Dear Mr Editor,

Yours faithfully

Surfaceman

Mr Editor

If you will kindly allow me a little of your valuable space, I would like to give Far East a hint he may possibly act upon. Let him try any railway labourer – in any of the lowest grades of course – and see how many he will get, from Berwick to Dunbar, who would leave his preasent work and return to the plough, even although he had a shilling less per week instead of being on level with the highest paid class of ploughmen – 2s above the average, and 4 above the lowest. In my opinion, there can be no comparison. A ploughman has to work, on the majority of farms, wet and dry, 60 hours weekly in the yolk – and has his stable work to do over and above Sunday and Saturday. He has no Saturday afternoon. If he is turned out at night to attend a horse that may have taken badly, he may possibly get a glass of whisky or a cup of tea, whereas a railway man turned out at night gets a day and a half paid him. Or, if on a Sunday, two *days pay. And if a good workman, he is treated with [...]. If any impudent puppit attacks him [he] has an appeal and, if he is right, the other soon finds his [own] level. Now, if a farmer, or his son, says, 'I want you to so-and-so' he must do it – or off he goes. It matters not at what time or season. Of course, there are old railway men at the plough, but they have mostly all been discharged for bad behaviour and saw nothing else but starvation staring him in the face. That's about the only thing ever sends any old hind back to the plough, but where he has often to submit quietly to the gibes and sneers of farmers' sons, who view him as a creature of another kind. Whose toil upheld their glittering show of Farmer's Son – who [is] to be met with, flying along the country roads in carriages with their sisters, off to Kirk or market. In fact, to any place where they can show to advantage. Or galloping on horseback like madmen, over hedge and ditch – mad drunk to the danger of the own and other people's lives. These are the class [the ploughman] has to submit to be taunted by when he is making an honest endeviours to raise himself. But, of course, such opposition only tends to bring sensible, practical men to their standard, who are eager to point out the way of [...]. Only the right men will come forward now, while the iron is hot, and strike. With many excuses for encroaching on your valuable space. I am,*

Yours Faithfully

Railway Man

Diary entry for Thursday, 21 February 1889

Would you kindly reminded the General Superintendent that I have never got this house cleaned and painted yet. His order has now been in the hand of the painter for four years, and the foreman has been at eight different times taking measurement. The last time I could not let him come, for reasons which I explained. So, he told me to let him know when it was convenient – which I did. That is now nine months ago. Also, that we cannot sit in the kitchen without the door open – for smoke – and we are all suffering more or less in consequence.

Meantime I am, sir, Faithfully Yours,

Andrew Ramage

Mr James Greenfield

Dear Sir

I beg to inform you that this house is in a deploreable state with smoke. The kitchen vent will not draw unless the door stands open and, as we have had trouble lately and have been compelled to keep it shut, we have all been nearly smoked out. Also, I beg to remind you that we have never got it papered and painted – as ordered by the General Superintendent four years ago. The foreman painter from Baileyfield has been here taking measurement three times. The last time I could not let him come for reasons which I explained to him at the time, and he said I was to let him know when it was conveanant for me, which I did. But there the matter rests at preasant. Now, Sir, if you would kindly lay these facts before the General Superintendent possibly it may have the desired effect, as I believe the preasant is generally the time for all inside work being done.

Yours Truly

Andrew Ramage

Diary entry for Wednesday, 13 March 1889

> *Rev Joseph Holmes*
> *Bloomsbury Mansions B_ Sq?*
> *London W le York Herald*

Diary entry for Sunday, 24 March 1889

> *Mary Jane McLean*
> *Thirlestane Castle*
> *Ettrick*
> *Selkirk*

Diary entry for Tuesday, 26 March 1889

> Procred Aloes 9.Grains
> Extract of Colveynth Coruprand 18.Do
> Caloniel 9.Do
> Tartarate of autineony 2.Do
> Made cut a mass & divided into 6 pills take 2 every 24 hours
>
> Dried sulphate of magnesia 6.drius
> Sulphate of Soda 3.Do
> Infusion of Sema 7 rincex
> Twelure of Jalip & compound twelure
> of cardamorus each ½ ounce
> 2 tablespoonfulls every 4 hours

Diary entry for Wednesday, 27 March 1889

> *Robert Begbie*
> *Gardiner*
> *Edinr 96*
> *Mr Angus Robertson* [brother-in-law]
> *C/of John Roberson Esq*
> *Emerdale Station*
> *Streatham Victoria*
> *Australia*

Diary entry for Tuesday, 2 April 1889

> *A Fulton and Tam McIlvenna*

Sir

*In your issue of last week you make a few remarks on the doings
and sayings at the Agricultural Society's meetins in your auld
borough toon of Haddington. How farmers can up in public
meetings and defend the present system of payment by gains
surpasses my comprehension. Mr Sideserf says when the plough
men cannot consume all his gains he gets the highest price from
the farmer. This may be so in his own case, but I can give him
instances of a farmer refuseing to give his man their just gains
when asked, but giving him instead money at the rate of 1/1 1d
per stair. Now, I ask, is that the highest prise or by what right
does he refuse the man his meal? The same farmer, with another
of his men, refused to give money and threw his meal down at
his door on the term morning when the man had no means of
disposing of it. Given this is one reason why ploughmen should
object to gains as if he had a supercadd money wage it would be
beyond the power of such mean masters to take advantage of the
men as they do. Mr Sideserf and the others know nothing of this,
but by conferring with them instead of bigoting them.*

...

Powdered Rhubarb 4 grains
Mercury & chalk 3 Do
Ginger in powder 1 Do

An alternative aperient for chie surd
Bran disket solution of Potash
30 drops twice a day in a wine
glass of Beer
No 1 7 : 18
Caloniel 1.grain
Powdered white sugar 2.Do
Made into powder & placed on the tongue every 2 or 3 hours.
Should the Caloniel act
on the bowels Powdered Kino instead of sugar
Inflamation of the Brain

Mr Thos McIlvenna
2 Osborne Ter
Portobello

List from inside front cover of second notebook

No 7637 Angus
No 1073 Willie
No 6083 Bob
No 1260 Lachie
Andrew Ramage
No 2185 James

Gateman
Stanhope lines
Biel Gates
Aldershot
Prestonkirk
Melaval

List from inside back cover of second notebook

Lowood
4.15 p.m.
William Kinnear
117 Alexander Street
Alexandria
Arteriosclerosis
3 Charlotte Square
Edinburgh

SY441
Rudge Moulton

Diary entry for Thursday, 6 August 1914

Biel Gates
Preston Kirk

Dear Jeanie

*This is a sad time with us here just now with the boys going away
and all this talk of war. Angus went past yesterday* [on] *midday for
London. Poor chap. Who knows, but it may be our last view of
him. It fairly knocked your mother up, but she is composed and
resigned to the will of God, who knows what is best. Willie is at
Dunbar but I hear they are going to York to relieve the Scotts
Grays* [Royal Scots Greys]. *We are all well here at present. Uncle
Rorie is staying with us for a day or two. He was in seeing Flo*
[Rorie's daughter] *on Tuesday. Lizzie* [Sandy's wife] *is coming for
Ella next week. I wish she was away as she is nervious about all
this talk of war. So as this is all my news I will conclude with
kindest love to you from us all.*

While I remain, your loving father.

Diary entry for Monday, 28 September 1914

No 7637 Pt A Ramage
LT Coy 2nd Scots Gds
20th Inf Brigade
Lyndhurst Camp
Hants, England

Dear Dad

*I received your welcome letter the day we left the Tower (about
ten days ago) and was pleased to see that you were all well etc.
We are down here at this place, which is about ten miles from
Southampton, going through about as rough a bit of training as
any man can stick. We don't know when we will sail but have to
be prepared to shift at any moment. I expect we will be off before
the end of next week. We have been waiting on the 2nd Gordons*

[Gordon Highlanders] *from Cairo – the same mob that relieved us out there. They arrived here last night so no doubt we will soon be out of it and into the thick of the scrap. I am in the pink myself and just wearying to get away as marching for days and digging trenches here, where it is not required, gets on my nerves. That's about all there is to say at present so will close with kindest love to all,*

while I remain your Affectionate Son,
Angus Ramage

Diary entry for Tuesday, 6 October 1914

S.S Cistrian
South Hampton

Dear Father and Mother,
It has come at last and we are on board ready for the road. We expect to sail this afternoon about 5.00 p.m. so we won't be long now before we see something of the Germans.

We have no idea where we will land and when we do I won't be able to let you know, but if you hear anything of the 7th Div[ision] *you will know I am there. We marched down here from Lyndhurst last night (It's about ten miles) and slept aboard this trooper. There is eight of them going with this lot so you may guess there is a good few troops. I have no more to say so I will say so long and wish you the best of health etc until I return if its the Lords will. Meantime,*

I remain your Affect Son
Angus Ramage

P.S. No 7637 Pt AR
L.T. Coy 2nd Scots Gds
20th Inft Brigade
British Expeditionary Force

Diary entry for Friday, 26 March 1915

> *Mrs H Inglis*
> *21 Newton Port*
> *Haddington*

Tuesday 11 May 1915

> 21 X 17

Diary entry for Friday, 28 May 1915

> 16 ¼ X 17 ⅛

List from inside front cover of third notebook

> *Andrew Ramage*
>
> 18 January 1916
> Angus 7637 [struck through] 26 Octr /14
> Willie 1073
> Bob 6083
> Jamie P.2185
> Lachie 1260 [first figure struck through] 325319
> M&J 174505
> W Ramage
> No 3 General Canadian Hospital
> France

List given following diary entry for 12 August 1916

> S 3017
> S 3669
> S 3948
> S 4245

S 4845
S P 640
S P 1160
W S 120

List from inside back cover of third notebook

11 ¼ X 8 ¼
65 /2

 4
280
100

80
100
547

Mr Dudgeon
Dalmeny
Royal
Royal

Diary entry for Sunday, 15 August 1915

1073
Heylesbury
Wiltshire

Diary entry for Friday, 9 February 1917

Robertson
1 Atholl Place

NOTES

All websites checked before going to press.

DSL   *Dictionary of the Scots Language*
SND   *Scottish National Dictionary*
OED   *Oxford English Dictionary*
NSA   *New Statistical Account of
        Scotland*

1   The spelling of this name is
    given variously as Sheils, Shiels,
    Shiles or Shields in the original
    notebooks. For consistency, the
    most frequently used spelling,
    Shiels, has been used through-
    out.

2   Dalkeith market was reputedly
    '… the greatest market for oats
    in the Kingdom' at this time,
    NSA, 1834–45, I 508: Edin-
    burghshire.

3   Grain sold by quarters were
    loads of 28olbs.

4   Broth in which cabbage was a
    principal ingredient; hence,
    broth or soup generally, *DSL*.

5   Dalkeith had a well-organised
    administration in place which
    included, 'a beneficial lease of
    the fair and market customs for
    which they are indebted to the
    liberality of His Grace the Duke
    of Buccleuch', *NSA*, 1834–45, I
    510: Edinburghshire. It may be
    that this arrangement meant
    that burgh taxes were lower
    than elsewhere.

6   One of the four days of the year
    legally marking the falling-due
    of certain payments, as rents,
    wages, etc., the settlement of
    business accounts, the com-
    mencement and expiry of leases,
    and of contracts of employment,
    esp. on farms. The four days
    were Candlemas (2 Feb.) Whit-
    sunday (15 May), Lammas
    (1 Aug.) and Martinmass (11
    Nov.). In 1886 the removal
    terms for house occupancy were
    fixed by statute as 28 May and
    28 November and these are
    commonly spoken of as terms,
    SND.

7   The covering of properly dis-
    posed straw with which the
    sloping top of a stack of corn or
    hay-rick is thatched, tidy, com-
    fortable, well-secured, in order,
    snug, *SND*.

8   The main beam or ridge of the
    roof, *SND*.

9   Scots proverb normally render-
    ed as 'Wha wul ti Cupar maun
    ti Cupar', meaning that there is
    little point in opposing one on a
    determined course of action.

10 71st (Highland) Light Infantry.

11 The Indian Rebellion of 1857,
    which began with a mutiny of

the sepoys of the East India Company's army in that year.

12 For 1861, the Worldwide Army Index (National Archive ref. WO12/7092) shows Stephen Ramage as Drummer/Fifer with 71st Fort (Highland) stationed at Sealkote, East Indies (now Siālkote, Pakistan). <http://search.www.findmypast. co.uk/search-world-records/1861-worldwide-army-index>

13 The use of the term friends here may suggest near relatives.

14 Bravery at this time would have meant fine, excellent and so the phrase might better be read as 'upholds that finery ...'.

15 Alternatively known as Torness Point, Firth of Forth.

16 Dalkeith seems a fair distance to travel and perhaps this was a special fair held only in certain locations. See Holmes, in Fenton and Veitch eds, 2011, 485.

17 An odd horse was an unpaired horse or orra horse. See Fenton, 2008, 100. The orra horse was kept for odd jobs, for gigs and odd jobs, SND.

18 Psoroptesovis, a form of allergic dermititus caused by the parasitic scab mite.

19 Calton jail was opened in 1817. Jules Verne, who visited Edinburgh in 1859, described the jail as resembling a small-scale version of a medieval town. Once the largest prison in Scotland, it had a reputation for being one of the hardest. It was demolished in 1930 leaving only the Governor's House and some of the original jail walls. <http://www.scotland.gov.uk/ About/Locations/St-Andrews-House-1/sah-70/caltonjail>

20 In each instance here, the term friend indicates a relative. In the case of the clothier, Mr Hunter, this is likely to be a brother or cousin on Andrew's mother's side of the family.

21 Registration of death only became compulsory in 1854 as a result of the Registration (Scotland) Act 1854. Failure to register a death could lead to a fine of up to £2.

22 This list omits William, who by this time was in Canada.

23 A scaur is a sheer rock, crag, precipice, cliff; a steep hill from which the soil has been washed away, DSL.

24 A workman who keeps a railway bed in repair.

25 Neighbouring was the practice of sharing labour to complete large tasks, e.g. harvesting.

26 Maybe Edin's Hall on the north-eastern slopes of Cockburn Law. Edin's Hall is comprised of the substantive remains of an iron-age broch built within the ramparts of an earlier fort.
See The Gazeteer for Scotland: <http://www.scottishplaces.info/ features/featurefirst10620.html>

27 Gunpowder mill and bomb factory at Roslin which closed in 1954 after 150 years of operation.

28 Runaway fairs were hiring fairs held a few days after main fairs which were held on the term

days. The purpose of the runaway fairs was to create an
opportunity for those who felt
they had made a poor bargain
to move on.

29 To harness a draught animal for
work. More generally to start
work of any kind in the morning, or after a break for food or
rest, *SND*.

30 Under pay = to be paid less than
required or deserved. Perhaps
here the reference is to Andrew
being paid as a child/youth
while doing an adult's share of
the work.

31 South Gyle was a farm on the
south side of the Gyle, Edinburgh.

32 Edinburgh Castle was a military
barrack at the time Andrew is
writing about, as was Piershill
and the Fort, Leith.

33 Cholera, typhus and small pox
were major killers in the nineteenth century and were the result of environmental pollution,
poverty and bad housing.
See Knox, online at:
<http://www.scran.ac.uk/
scotland/pdf/SP2_3Health.pdf>

34 Along with flour milling, timber
import and finishing remained a
notable industry in Leith at the
beginning of the 20th century.
See, Russell, 1922, ch. 32.

35 Green wood is recently felled
wood that has not been dried.

36 Probably Caledonian Railway;
this line opened in 1874.

37 A dark-coloured soap made
from alkali and animal fat or
fish oil, *OED*.

38 Copper sulphate used to treat
sores and skin ulcers.

39 Getting my gong, meant to be
summoned or called upon to
stop. Here the meaning is probably laid off.

40 Andrew worked as a carter for
a number of firms during his
time at Leith.

41 Distilling and bottling were
notable industries in Leith
during this period and beyond.

42 A large earthenware or stone-
ware jug or jar, used for holding
spirits, *OED*.

43 This is likely to be a reference
to the horse tram-cars which
became popular following the
first Edinburgh Street Tramway
Act (1871) which authorised
the construction of ten separate
lines in and around the city. The
tramcars carried 40–50 passen-
gers, twice as many as the horse-
omnibuses. See Freeman, in
Fenton and Veitch eds, 2009,
414.

44 A weir on the Water of Leith.

45 CDV = *carte de visite*. Card-
mounted photograph. These
cards, mostly portraits, were
produced and sold by professional photographers and gained
popularity from the mid-1800s.

46 Angus, Isabella's youngest
sibling, emigrated to Australia
in 1885 and never returned to
Scotland. He settled in the Mel-
bourne area, married and raised
a family. He died in 1945.

47 Half a sovereign was a coin with
the value of ten shillings.

48 For a detailed discussion of the

49 formation and activities of the Scottish Farm Servants' Union, see Anthony, 1997, 119–43.

49 The ganger was the foreman of a work gang.

50 At one time New Year was the main festival in the Scottish calender while Christmas was largely ignored. This feeling dated from the aftermath of the Reformation when Christmas was condemned as papist.

51 Guising was a Hogmanay cele-bration where the young folk and children would dress up and go round the houses making a small performance at each with the expectation of reward of food or drink. This was a popu-lar New Year pastime in com-munities across Scotland and continues in some places today.

52 Handsel Monday was the first Monday of the new year, on which handsel (a gift) was given. Formerly a holiday, *SND*.

53 George Ernest Jean-Marie Boulanger (1837–1891) was a French general and politician.

54 This is a reference to the pain Andrew experienced following the amputation of his right arm.

55 A light dusting of snow, or frost.

56 The land of the leel (leal) was the home of the blessed after death, heaven.

57 Registration of death became compulsory under the Registra-tion of Births, Deaths and Marriages (Scotland) Act 1854, s. 38. Deaths had to be notified to the Registrar within eight days of death or a fine of one pound

was imposed. See, Crowther and Cameron, in Mulhern ed., 2012, 659.

58 By this time William had moved to Saskatchewan, and the letter did eventually reach him.

59 Irish Home Rule was a topic of vociferous political debate during much of the latter half of the nineteenth century and beyond. This debate was widely reported in the newspapers and periodicals of the day. Sir William Harcourt was, at the time of writing, a leading Glad-stonian Liberal and was putting the case in favour of Home Rule. See Stansky, 'Harcourt, Sir William George Granville Venables Vernon (1827–1904)', *Oxford Dictionary of National Biography*, online edition, 2008: <http://www.oxforddnb.com/view/article/33693>

60 Working block refers to the 'time interval' system used to manage the progress of trains from one section of track to another.

61 Prior to the outbreak of WWI the level of withdrawals from banks was such that on Friday 31 July 1914 all banks closed for one week. See Roberts, 2013.

62 Lord Binning (1856–1917) was the eldest son of George Baillie-Hamilton-Arden. After a long military career he retired from the army in 1907 but remained in the Territorial Force and served as Commanding Officer of the Lothian and Border Horse Yeomanry.

63 The battle of Heligoland Bight was the first naval battle of the war.

64 Lachie was born 29/10/1897 so was only 16 when he enlisted.

65 Hedderwick is near Dunbar. Nearby Hedderwick Links provided ideal terrain for military training and has a long history of being used in this way.

66 Reference to enteric fever, commonly known as typhoid.

67 This may refer to a machine used to make mash for animal feed, or for distilling.

68 The Co-operative Societies across the UK paid their members a share of the profits as a dividend. This was colloquially known as the 'divi'. The term divide, used by Andrew, is most likely a ref. to this dividend.

69 To take or receive in the church, especially for the first time after a wedding, birth or funeral, or the appointment of a civil or academic body. A ceremonial church attendance, *SND*.

70 The *Emden* was a German raider which was sunk on 9 November 1914 by HMAS *Sydney*. It is possible that in referring to *Kharbrush*, Andrew may have had in mind the bombardment, siege and capture of Kiaochow (Jiaozhou) Bay by the Japanese on 7 November 1914.

71 The kirn was a celebration with feasting and dancing, to mark the conclusion of cutting the corn or the end of harvest, *SND*.

72 This was during the first battle of Ypres.

73 Lady Frances Balfour (1858–1931) was a Liberal and a supporter of William Gladstone and of women's suffrage. The Balfour family home was in East Lothian and Frances is buried at Whittinghame.

74 This refers to the battle of Dogger Bank.

75 This suggests the available house was a farmworker's cottage.

76 A panel doctor was one who was paid for from the receipts of National Insurance (NI) which was introduced in 1911. Having contributed National Insurance, Andrew was eligible to see a NI panel doctor at no charge.

77 St Cuthbert's was a Co-operative Society founded in Edinburgh in 1859. It continues in trade today as SCOTMID, the largest independent co-operative society in Scotland.

78 Someone who repairs saw and sawmill equipment.

79 2/8, 3/8, 2/5 are Battalion numbers: e.g. 2/8 would be 8th Battalion, 2nd Line.

80 Most likely a reference to Pittencrieff Park and The Glen.

81 The 1250-foot Portobello Pier opened in 1871. The many attractions included a seaward-end concert hall. The pier was demolished in 1917 following its closure due to the high cost of maintaining the structure.

82 During WWI, travel was highly restricted. Andrew is here referring to a pass for travel outwith his locality.

83 Military Mounted Police.

84 Kirkcaldy is known as the Lang Toon because it stretches along the front facing the Forth estuary. Sir Michael Nairn began the manufacture of linoleum in the town in the late 19th century.

85 This refers to one of several sets of gates into the Dalmeny Estate. These gates can still be seen.

86 Lady Clementine Waring and her husband, Major Walter Banff, converted their home in Berwickshire into a convalescent home for officers. She did a great deal to support soldiers and helped many to recover from the horrors of shell shock.

87 A state pension was introduced following passage of the Old Age Pensions Act 1908. Receiving the pension was colloquially known as 'receiving your Lloyd George' after Lloyd George, the Chancellor of the Exchequer at the time the legislation was enacted.

88 The Derby Scheme was introduced in 1915 to encourage men to enlist voluntarily with the reward that they would only be called up when necessary. This scheme proved unsuccessful and was given up in December of the same year.

89 Powderhall Races and Sports. From 1909 the Powderhall marathon was run as a road race from Falkirk to Powderhall. By 1916, the race was run on the cinder track at the stadium and eventually given up altogether in 1943. Events included the Powderhall New Year Carnival for professional runners.

90 The first part of this journey would have been made by electric tramway which, by 1909, extended as far as Port Seton. The second part is likely to have been by a vehicle drawing on cable traction which, by 1902, had widely replaced the old horse tramway system. See Freeman, in Fenton and Veitch eds, 2009, 424.

91 This may refer to the register kept by the 'Registry Office for Servants' which acted as an agent between employers and workers. See Holmes, in Fenton and Veitch eds, 2011, 449.

92 The Battle of Verdun was the longest battle of WWI.

93 On the night of 2 November 1916, Edinburgh was attacked during Zeppelin raids: see <http://www.edinburghs-war. ed.ac.uk/city-defences/zeppelin-raids-over-edinburgh>

94 The Guards' Society may have been one of the many trade societies which provided assistance for their workers.

95 Operational from September 1915, East Fortune was commissioned in 1914 as part of an initiative to provide a string of home defence airfields along the eastern seaboard, from Edinburgh to the south-east coast of England.

96 Actually thirty-three years since Andrew lost his arm.

97 Aqua was a term sometimes

used to refer to whisky, see
SND.

98 The Field Card was a rather
crude form of censorship used
by the military to encourage
soldiers to send only the most
basic information home. The
cards were printed with a number of multiple-choice options
and the sender then deleted the
options which were unnecessary. Instructions on the card
advised the soldier that nothing
was to be written on the card
except a signature and date.
There was also a note stating
that 'If anything else is added
the card will be destroyed'.
<http://www.bbc.co.uk/guides/
zqtmyrd>

99 In 1916–17 a concentration of
over 500,000 British, French
and Serbian troops was based in
Salonika (Macedonia) when an
epidemic of malaria broke out
in the town, which came to be
known as the 'Bird Cage', and
its environs. Of the 300,000
British and French troops,
around 120,000 (40%) became

unfit for active service due to
malaria. Allied with other dis-
eases, at one point it reduced
the strength of the Allied force
to only 100,000 effectives.
<http://www.westernfront
association.com/great-war-on-
land/casualties-medcal/693-
malaria-in-the-war.html>

100 A colloquial expression meaning for a fight or a sharp alter-
cation, see *OED*.

101 A perquisite, an allowance in
kind in addition to cash wages,
SND.

102 Patent medicines was a term
used to describe medicines which
were invented and sold as original, often to a secret recipe to
avoid imitation. Some were the
forerunners of modern-day
over-the-counter medicines, but
many were proven to have no
effect whatsoever. Patent medicine vendors were often known
as snake oil vendors.
<http://www.sciencemuseum.
org.uk/broughttolife/techniques/
patent.aspx>

BIOGRAPHICAL NOTES

Andrew Ramage

Andrew was born on 15 February 1854, at Dodridge Farm, Ormiston, East Lothian, the youngest of nine children born to Alexander Ramage (1809–89) and Mary Hunter (1812–68).

He attended various schools, including House O'Muir, Pathhead and Temple, until aged 12 years. Thereafter he worked on farms, first in Berwickshire and then Midlothian. He moved to Leith, aged 15, to work as a carter, and then from age 18 as a (horse-drawn) lorry-driver between Leith Docks and breweries. Before the age of 24, he started work with North British Railways as a Goods Guard at Portobello.

Andrew married Isabella McBain Robertson on 7 June 1878 at Portobello, Midlothian. Ten children were born between 1879 and 1897, three eldest at Portobello and seven youngest at Biel Crossing, East Linton, East Lothian. Following the loss of his arm after an accident at work, he was appointed Gatekeeper at Biel Crossing near East Linton and remained there until retirement in 1915. He then moved to Craigie, Dalmeny, West Lothian, where he died on 25 September 1917 aged 63 years.

Isabella McBain Robertson

Isabella was born on 20 May 1858 at Belses Railway Station House, Roxburghshire. She was the fifth of six children born to Alexander Robertson (1818–94) and Jane Morrison Cameron (1831–99). Her father was the railway station master at Belses.

The family also spent time in Rothes, Moray and then at Portobello. Isabella remained at Craigie with daughter Jean after Andrew's death in 1917. In the early 1920s she moved to Dalmeny village with Jean. The unmarried sons often worked away.

Isabella died on 10 August 1933 aged 75 years, at Dalmeny, West Lothian.

Alexander Ramage (son)

Alexander (Sandy) was born on
22 October 1879 at Portobello,
Midlothian. Alexander was the
eldest of ten children born to
Andrew and Isabella. He attended
school at Tyninghame, East
Lothian and went on to work as a
railway stoker in Edinburgh.

He married Elizabeth
McDonald on 19 December 1902,
at Canongate, Edinburgh. They
had five children (born between
1904 and 1920). The two eldest
were born in Edinburgh and the
youngest three in Cheshire, where
Sandy was employed on Capesthorn estate (his job included
chauffeur duties).

He served as an army staff
driver during WWI and in 1916
was posted to France. He returned
to Edinburgh in the 1920s and
thereafter worked as a garage
foreman and general dealer. He
died on 15 September 1937, aged
57 years, at the Royal Infirmary,
Edinburgh.

Duncan Ramage (son)

Duncan (Dow) was born on 31
May 1881 at Portobello and
attended school at Tyninghame,
East Lothian. He died on 5 June
1892, aged 11 years. The cause of
death was cerebral meningitis.
Family lore held that this illness
followed a fall from a tree.

George Ramage (son)

George (Dod) was born on 29
October 1882 and attended school
at Tyninghame, East Lothian.
He emigrated to Canada in 1902
where he worked for his uncle,
William Ramage, at Kelso,
Saskatchewan.

In January 1903, he received
entry for his own homestead NE
10-11-33 W1 at Walpole near
Wawota, Saskatchewan, and
patent for his own homestead in
November 1907.

He married Margaret Hazel
Campbell on 14 September 1910,
in Wawota, Saskatchewan. They
had 15 children between 1911
and 1933: one son died in infancy.
In December 1928 he travelled to
Scotland, with brothers Andrew
and James, to visit family, and then
returned to Wawota in February
1929.

He retired to Winnipeg, Manitoba in 1952 and died there on
27 December 1957 aged 75 years.

Jean Morrison Cameron Ramage (daughter)

Jean was born on 21 March 1885
and attended school at Tyninghame, East Lothian. She worked
as a domestic servant in a number
of places, including Edinburgh,
Dumfries & Galloway and Inver-
urie.

In 1915 she moved to Craigie
with her parents and then later to

Dalmeny village with her mother. From home she ran the village shop until her retirement and she remained in Dalmeny until her death at the Royal Infirmary, Edinburgh, on 16 August 1957, aged 72 years.

Andrew Ramage (son)

Andrew was born on 18 August 1886 and attended school at Tyninghame, East Lothian.

He worked on Biel Estate and at Knowes market garden before emigrating to Canada in 1906.

He worked for his brother George and other farmers around Wawota and Kelso, Saskatchewan and then at Solsgirth, Manitoba. He received entry for his own homestead, NW ¼ of Section 19, in Township 9, Range 3, West of the 3rd Meridian, at Melaval, Saskatchewan in April 1909 and patent for his own homestead in April 1913.

In December 1922 he travelled to Scotland to visit family, returned to Melaval in February 1923.

Andrew married Anna Emma Moore (widow) in 1923, at Melaval, Saskatchewan, Canada. One child was born in 1924, but died of complications following vaccination immediately prior to a planned visit to Scotland in 1928.

In December 1928 Andrew travelled to Scotland with Anna, stepdaughter Lena Depew and brothers George and James, to visit family. He returned to Melaval in March 1929.

Anna died in 1939 and he later married Martha Myrtle Dodge on 2 June 1941 in Regina, Canada. Two children were born between 1943 and 1944.

Andrew died on 25 December 1960 aged 74 years, in Regina, Canada.

Angus Robertson Ramage (son)

Angus was born on 13 March 1888 and attended school at Tyninghame, East Lothian.

He listed and served as a Guardsman in the Scots Guards, 2nd Battalion and in 1910 was based at Caterham, Surrey. In 1911/12 he was based in Cairo, Egypt.

Angus left the army to join the Linlithgowshire Police, but received an immediate recall to the Scots Guards upon outbreak of WWI in August 1914. He sailed on 5 October 1914 aboard SS *Cistrian* from Southampton to Zeebrugge, Belgium, and was Killed in Action at Gheluvelt, Ypres, Belgium, on 26 October 1914, aged 26 years.

William (Bill) Hunter Ramage (son)

Bill was born on 1 December 1889 and attended school at Tyninghame, East Lothian.

He worked on the Biel Estate before joining the Territorial Army, Lothian & Border Horse, about 1906. He was called-up immediately upon the outbreak of WWI, and in November 1915 he was sent with the regiment via France to Serbia, and then to Salonika, Greece for Bulgarian campaign.

Bill married Katherine Patricia Bennett Keegan on 5 August 1922, St Giles, Edinburgh, and together they had four children born between 1923 and 1927.

After retirement, he remained in East Linton until 1971 when he and Katherine emigrated to Canada to join their youngest son in Vancouver, British Columbia. Bill died there on 19 March 1976, aged 86 years.

Robert (Bob) McLauchlan Ramage (son)

Bob was born on 5 April 1892 and attended school at Tyninghame, East Lothian.

He served his apprenticeship with McArthur's joiners, East Linton and thereafter worked as a journeyman joiner around East Lothian.

In May 1915 Bob listed in the Royal Flying Corps as a carpenter, first at Gosport, Hampshire. In March 1916 he was posted to France with No. 22 Squadron. After WWI continued working as journeyman joiner.

Bob married Helen Young on 8 November 1922, at Armadale, West Lothian, and together they had two children, born between 1923 and 1933. He set up business as a master joiner (later including funeral undertaking).

After retirement Bob remained at Armadale. He died on 20 October 1976, aged 84 years, at Bangour General Hospital, West Lothian.

James (Jim) Ramage (son)

Jim was born on 7 May 1894 and attended school at Tyninghame, East Lothian.

He became a policeman at Haddington, East Lothian, before being enlisted to the Military Mounted Police in October 1915. In December 1915 Jim was serving at Alexandria, Egypt, and later (November 1916) at Salonika, Greece.

Following WWI, he returned to the police force at Prestonpans, East Lothian, before emigrating to Canada in June 1922. Initially, he worked for his brothers, George and Andrew, and in later years spent the summers working on farms at Standard, Alberta, and winters working for Corps of Commissioners (commercial security) in Calgary.

In December 1928 he travelled to Scotland with his brothers George and Andrew, to visit family and returned to Calgary in March 1929.

At the outbreak of WWII, Jim listed in the Canadian Army, Provost Corps, as RSM. He served in England and visited family when on leave.

Jim returned to Calgary, July 1943, on prisoner escort duty and for leave. He died shortly afterwards, on 24 July 1943, aged 49 years.

Lauchlan (Lachie, Lauchie) Robertson Ramage (son)

Lachie was born on 29 October 1897 and attended school at Tyninghame, East Lothian.

Aged 16, in September 1914, he listed in the Royal Scots. In November 1914 he was posted to France with the Royal Scots 8th Battalion. He returned to Scotland in February 1915 following respi-

ratory disease and was thereafter based in Peebles, Edinburgh, Falkirk and Chelmsford before being posted to Ireland in January 1917.

In June of the same year Lachie returned to France with the Royal Scots 12th Battalion.

In October 1918 his actions resulted in the award of a Distinguished Conduct Medal.

After WWI, Lachie returned to Dalmeny, and in November 1932 he married Mary McPherson, Dalmeny, West Lothian. Together they had six children, born between 1933 and 1945. The family moved to Roseburn, Edinburgh and worked in business in the Dean Village, Edinburgh, manufacturing and installing shop shutters.

Lauchlan died on 18 February 1957 aged 59 years, in the Royal Infirmary, Edinburgh.

BIBLIOGRAPHY

Anthony, R. *Herds and Hinds: Farm Labour in Lowland Scotland, 1900–1939*, East Linton, 1997.

Crowther, A. and Cameron, A. Civil Registration: The Law and the Individual in Scotland since 1854. In Mulhern, M. (ed.), *The Law* (Scottish Life and Society: A Compendium of Scottish Ethnology), vol. 13, Edinburgh, 2012, 655–71.

Dictionary of the Scots Language: <http://www.dsl.ac.uk/dsl/>

Fenton, A. Farm Workers before and after the Agricultural Improvement Period. In Mulhern, M., Beech, J., and Thompson, E. (eds), *The Working Life of the Scots* (Scottish Life and Society: A Compendium of Scottish Ethnology), vol. 7, Edinburgh, 2008, 87–106.

Freeman, M. Urban Transport in the Nineteenth Century. In Fenton, A. and Veitch, K. (eds), *Farming and the Land* (Scottish Life and Society: A Compendium of Scottish Ethnology) vol. 8, Edinburgh, 2009, 407–35.

Holmes, H. Seasonal and Casual Agricultural Workers. In Fenton, A. and Veitch, K. (eds), *Farming and the Land* (Scottish Life and Society: A Compendium of Scottish Ethnology), vol. 2, Edinburgh, 2011, 477–502.

Knox, W. W. A History of the Scottish People – Health in Scotland 1840–1940: <http://www.scran.ac.uk/scotland/pdf/SP2_3Health.pdf>

Oxford English Dictionary, <http://www.oed.com/> [subscription service]

Roberts, R. *Saving the City: The Great Financial Crisis of 1914*, Oxford, 2013.

Russell, J. *The Story of Leith*, London, 1922.

Stansky, P. 'Harcourt, Sir William George Granville Venables Vernon (1827–1904)', *Oxford Dictionary of National Biography*, Oxford, 2004; online edn, Jan 2008: <http://www.oxforddnb.com/view/article/33693>

The Statistical Accounts of Scotland Online, 1791–1845, <http://edina.ac.uk/stat-acc-scot/> [subscription service]

GLOSSARY

aff off, away from
aiblins perhaps
antebellum happening in the time before war
arrove arrived
auld old
awa away
aye yes, always
bacca, baccy tobacco
bairn infant child
bairnies little children
baith both
bang stick bang chain – for fastening a load of heavy logs
bannock round flat cake of oat-barley or peas-meal, baked on a girdle
banter teasing, rebuke, badinage
beating to strike (bushes, undergrowth etc.) in order to rouse game
belt a blow, or a hit, surround, encircle
ben in or towards the inner part of a house
bide remain, stay, reside, await
bit a small piece, part of the bridle that sits in the horse's mouth
blate bashful, timid, diffident, modest

blaw blow
bob one shilling
bog mossy ground
bogie a kind of coarse, black tobacco of a medium twist, a small railway freight truck
boll a dry measure of weight or capacity varying according to commodity and locality
bondage service due from a farmworker to a farmer
bondager a person who performs bondage service, chiefly a female field-worker supplied by a farm-tenant in accordance with the conditions of his tenancy
bonny beautiful, pretty
bot check, bump, punch
bounden bound
brae road with a steep gradient
brake to go twice over ground with the harrow, the first time this instrument is applied
braw brave, fine, splendid
bray brae, hill

breeks trousers
brick a country lad
brig bridge
broonie benevolent sprite, supposed to perform household tasks in the night
broth thick soup made from mutton, barley and vegetables; also to sweat profusely
bruit brute
bubbly jack cry baby
burn stream
bust broken, of spirit
but and ben both the inner and outer parts
butt a ridge or strip of ploughed land
cadge beg, sponge
cadger chancer, sponger
canny can't
canty lively, cheerful, pleasant
cauld cold
chaff the mass of husks, etc. separated from the seeds during threshing. Also ref. to straw or chopped hay used to stuff cloth mattresses
chiel child, a lad, (young) man, a young woman

cohabit dwell together as husband and wife
cossey warm and comfortable
couped toppled over
crack talk, gossip, conversation
cronies old women (derogatory), old friends
cryed called for, summoned
cuddy a horse or donkey
cudgel a short, stout stick, 'take up the cudgel' – to join in a dispute, especially to defend oneself or another
cuss curse
darg a day's work
dear expensive
dint chance, occasion, opportunity
dook duck, bathe, soaking
doon down
dram a small drink of liquor
drap drop
drill to sow in rows
drive to carry through
drookin soaking, drenching
dyke a wall
fair the gathering for buying and selling, or hiring (of farm workers)
farl a three-cornered oatcake, the fourth part of a bannock
farrant grumpy
feart afraid
fine comfortable, contented, having had enough; or very well

flit remove, transport from one place to another, move house
fly cunning
frae from
fretted worried
fur for
furlough leave of absence, especially from military duty
gaffer chargehand, foreman, boss
gang go, went
gatherin gathering
gauled galled, resentful
gey very
gibbles tools, implements, articles, wares
gig two-wheeled carriage
gin if, whether
glen a valley or hollow, chiefly one traversed by a stream, and frequently narrow and steep-sided
graip an iron-pronged fork used in farming and gardening – graiping
greasy unctuous or oily in manner
grieve the overseer or head-workman on a farm, a farm-bailiff
guid good, worthy, respectable
hae have
hag derogatory term for a woman of a mean disposition
hame home
hard up short of money, or anything else, e.g. health
harried plundered, harassed, destroyed
harrow a spiked frame,

or other contrivance for breaking up or levelling soil, covering seed, etc.
haugh a piece of level ground on the banks of a river
hawked bargained, sold
hind a farm-servant, a ploughman
hiring fair a fair or market held for the purpose of hiring farm workers
hirpled limped, hobbled
howdie a midwife, a woman who lays out the dead
howler amusing, producing a laugh
huff sulk
hussy an impudent girl; a promiscuous or worthless girl or woman
ilka each, every
jacks rabbits
janker a long pole on wheels used to transport chiefly timber suspended under it
jings expression of surprise
ken know, known
keipt keep, look after, kept
kirk church
kist chest, trunk, large box
knock a blow
knocked-up exhausted, tired out
lad male, youth
laird the landlord of landed property or an estate
laith loathe, reluctant
lang long

lank of lean stature
lash a blow, physical or verbal
lassie a girl, a maiden
lave the rest, the remainder
law a rounded, usually conical hill, often isolated or conspicuous
leading in carry (harvested grain or hay) home from the field
lighter flat-bottomed boat, barge
list enlisted (into the army)
lobby hall
loon lad
lowse free, unrestrained, unconstructed
mains the home farm of an estate; the outbuildings of a farm
manse the dwelling-house provided for the parish minister
masher this probably refers to a machine used to create a mixture e.g. of bran with meal or turnips, which was beaten and stirred to produce food for animals
meat food in general, for men or animals
midden domestic rubbish, refuse heap
mind remember, remind, look after
mournings black garments worn to show grief
muddle untidy
nae not
nane neither

neb nose
neer-do-well good for nothing, a rake, debauchee
nip measure of [whisky]
no not
o'er over
ony any
out-by outside, out in the fields, field labourer
pailing fencing
peeler policeman
phisic liquid medicine
pooin pulling
poorin poring
poultice soft, moist mass of material, typically used to relieve soreness or inflammation and kept in place with a cloth
prood proud
quail to fail in spirit
quines girl, young woman
rake an accumulation, load, hoard, what has been gathered together
range fire grate
reduce set aside by legal process, to annul
rhone pipe the pipe or gutter at the eaves of a roof designed to carry off rain water
riled aggravated
roup sell or let by public auction
rue pitiable
sa so
sair sore
sang song
sark a man's shirt, a woman's shift or chemise
selt sold

scoogin sheltering from (the rain)
shanked send off on foot, dismiss
shebang primitive dwelling
sheebeen unlicensed drinking premises
sic such, of such a kind
singling thin out (seedlings, esp. turnips)
skirted go by the edge of
sly secretly
sneck-drawin guileful, artfulness
snipe wading bird
snotty short-tempered, curt
soger soldier
sojurn a digression
speerin questioning
sprigg small wooden peg
star name for various kinds of grass or sedge, usually growing in moorish or boggy ground
stay dwell, reside, make one's home
steel a steep bank, especially a spur on a hill ridge
stray porter casual worker, porter
supercadd add as extra
syne since then
tackit a hobnail used to stud the soles of shoes
tae to
taen taken
tattie potato
telt told
themsel themselves
thole suffer, have to bear; endure with

patience or fortitude,
put up with, tolerate

toom empty, unoccu-
pied, vacant

toon town

tow rope, cord, length
of strong twine,
string, etc.

traivis a board, shutter,
or the like, used as a
check or stop for a
load on a cart

trap a light carriage

turbit domestic pigeon

twa two

unco strange, awful

virago violent or bad-
tempered woman

vituperative bitter,
abusive

wad would

waft gentle movement
of air

wall a natural spring of
water which forms a
pool or stream

wassie smart, clever

wean a small child,
especially a young
one

wee small, young

wha who

whin the common furze
or gorse

wi with

wifie affectionate term
for a female friend,
wife

wile pass time in a
leisurely manner

woefu woeful

wreath bank of snow,
or drift, probably
originally an accumu-
lation of swirls of
snow

wrought worked

ye you

INDEX